Walking Backwards

My Life In the News
By Betty Hansen
Compiled by Holly Tiret

LULU PRESS

Walking Backwards Copyright © 2016 by Betty Hansen.

Dedication

This book is dedicated to my entire, very large and loving family. My mom, for providing a rich written history of our lives. My dad, Herbert James Hansen Sr. (1913-1976), for being the steadfast family man and progressive thinker who was not only okay with the idea of a 'working woman' back in the day, but also for the immense amount of pride he had for my mom. My six brothers, Herbert James Hansen Jr., Ralph Wayne Hansen, Stephen Andrew Hansen, John Christopher Hansen, Edward James Hansen (1952-2009), and Joseph Gerard Hansen and my two sisters, Barbara Sue (Hansen) Schultz (1957-2000) and Patricia Ann (Hansen) Jaime. We are all in the book, either directly or indirectly providing 'material' for mom to write about. Thank goodness, she had and still has a sense of humor! As I re-typed the articles, it seems a wonder we all survived, and still are able to laugh and sometimes cry remembering moments captured forever in her writing.

In addition to my brothers and sisters, I would like to dedicate this book to my extensive extended family. I am not sure my parents realized when they married that they were the start of a huge, loving tribe. Our family has grown so large in numbers it takes renting a hall to have a total family get together. Last count (living) 112 from 7 children (7 spouses), 30 'home-made' grandchildren (16 spouses), 6 'ready-made' grandchildren (5 spouses), 30 'home-made' great grandchildren and 11 'ready-made great-grandchildren.

I would also like to thank the Saginaw News for giving my mom the platform for creating all of her articles that she shared with so many people for so many years.

Chapter 3: Marriage 61

Chapter 4: Parenting 72

Elizabeth Marie (Morningstar) Hansen

Introduction

It still surprises me when I realize I am a mother of nine children and a writer. When I was a little girl, after I had rid myself of the delusion that I was in reality a princess, I decided when I grew up I'd be a rich and famous movie star with no children at all.

I really didn't want to be a writer. That's what my mother was. Nobody wants to be like their mother. That's what my teachers in school said I'd be with my big imagination. No child wants to be what big people want them to be. I became a mother as a natural result of marriage mixed with carelessness, and, after I'd been one for a while decided it was very enjoyable.

I became a writer because my husband worked nights and I had a typewriter in the house I inherited from my grandmother. I fooled around with it and wrote an article – my observation that parents rely too much on outside advice instead of their own God-given instincts for parenting.

I showed it to my mother who told me how to prepare it for marketing and sent it off to a magazine called "Extension," a Catholic publication devoted to family life. They sent me a check for $100 which changed the whole course of my married life.

My husband, practical man that he was realized I might be a potential gold mine and from then on not only did not stand in the way of my writing, kept encouraging me to go at it. This was a real departure from tradition in those days when a good wife was supposed to put such talents aside in favor of cooking, cleaning and taking care of kids.

My dad taught me how to read before I went to school by helping me sound out words in newspaper headlines. When I started Kindergarten I could read things like, "Chicago gangland slaying," and "Lindbergh flies the Atlantic," which upset the teachers of that day to no end. They were still teaching first graders to read, "I am a gingerbread boy." School was never a great experience as a result.

My parents were people who, for the most part, were pretty absorbed in their own lives. They also were bringing me up in a new era of child psychology which said that being strict was detrimental to a child's creativity. As a result I didn't receive the discipline I probably should have had and it's been a problem all my life. I have to drive myself to do the ordinary day-to-day things other people take for granted.

Left to myself, which I actually am now, and lacking any motivation, I could very easily revert to being the undisciplined, lazy little creature I was at age 9.

On the other hand, being ignored left me a lot of time for daydreaming and reading books in a family library that usually covered a couple of walls in any house we ever lived in. since nobody bothered to say read this or that, I started at one end of the shelf and read my way through to the end. School, after all this, was always dull, which was mostly why I got bored and left it in the 11th grade.

There was always a chance that my father would be transferred to another city so we lived in rented houses for almost the entire time until I married and left home. For one reason or another, we moved a lot with the result that I was always the new kid in six different elementary schools.

Being the new kid can be an advantage later in life. Now that I'm living in a different state, 2,000 miles from where I grew up, I am still a new kid and always find it sort of a fun challenge. The idea is to see how fast one can make friends, fit into the environment and become an old kid.

But I sometimes miss not having deeper roots. Like a lot of people I can't point to the house where I grew up, to the church in which I was baptized and married, to school friends who knew me from kindergarten through high school. I've thought a lot about this and come to the conclusion that, except for the years I spent on Brown Street raising my kids, my mission is to be a nomad.

When the first of my children were babies, Grandma Hansen, who liked kids best at that age, would say, "You don't know it now, but this is the happiest time of your life – when they're all little."

I saw it differently. There wasn't a time in my children's lives that they did not delight me with new aspects of what it is to be growing human beings at any point of life – from the moment a baby first holds up his or her head, to their own adulthood.

Looking back, I don't believe I was a perfect parent. There are a lot of things I'd do differently, but life is one big scene you don't rehearse for and you don't get a second chance so I don't grieve over it too much. My children grew up to be perfectly delightful human beings.

Like a lot of other parents, generations of them, in fact, I tried to be the sort of parent I'd have liked to have had. I am sure my kids probably do the same thing. I tried to have time to listen to them, to read to them and be present in both spirit and body when they needed me. Sometimes I succeeded, sometimes I didn't. That's the way of life.

When I met my husband he had just gone to work in the inspection department at Saginaw Steering Gear following a layoff. He'd started there in 1938. But in 1940 things were looking a little better except the young people were talking about how soon it would be before war broke out and all the draft age men would go into the armed forces.

Saginaw was peaceful place to live and sort of a fun place in which to be young. Saturday night was the high spot of the week. We'd gather our particular group of friends together and take a bus downtown, unless one of us was lucky enough to have a car for the night. There were no less than a dozen places downtowns where there was live music for dancing. We'd go from place to place – the guys in their group, or groups the girls in their own little gangs. When everyone was finally paired off and a sufficient number of automobiles commandeered we'd head out to the roadhouses on the edge of town.

My problem was that I was only 16 and the other girls warned me to lie and tell the inevitable policeman at the door I was 18.

It was in this situation that I met Herb, my future husband. He came in with his friends, some of whom knew my friends. He sat down beside me and I decided right then I was falling in love. It being leap year, I asked him to marry me, just kiddingly, of course. He said okay, then laughed and said he never planned to get married.

I said, "Well, you're safe with me because I don't want to get married either."

This was the Saturday before Palm Sunday in 1940. A year later, on March 29, 1941 we were married. I was just 17 and he was 26. There was a war looming in our future and we decided we'd spend what little time we probably had left together.

He was a very shy guy but very good looking. I remember thinking the first time I saw him that he'd probably have awfully cute children with his brown eyes, long eyelashes and dimpled chin. Now I see so many of his looks in each one of my children and smile to remember how right on I was when I chose a mate at so young an age.

14

As it turned out, Herb didn't go to war. He was deferred from military service on two counts – he had asthma and was employed in key military production.

I think he tried very hard to be a good father to his kids. I once met a company representative, a man who called on him when he worked in the design lab at Steering Gear. He said, "I never knew a guy who loved his kids so much. He was so proud of them. Every time I stopped in he had another one to brag about."

He could fix anything mechanical in the entire world. I never knew what it was to have so much as a broken toaster that he couldn't repair.

We weave the design

"I often think that people we love and the people who love us, not only make us more human, but they become part of us, to carry forever, whether we see them or not. In some ways we are a sum total of who we are." (Author unknown)

This paragraph was given to me by a friend. It reminded me not only of people I have loved but times and places.

Never an October passes that I do not remember hanging clothes in my backyard, hearing the Saginaw High band at practice in Alumni Field across the street.

Now there is a new school there and the field rarely used. But Saginaw High band practice was the high spot of a bright fall day for me in 1951.

There were the days when I spent endless hours in telephone conversations with friends while the babies played with the pots and pans on the kitchen floor. And the coffee times...do housewives still do this? Or has it gone the way of liberated womanhood?

I can't say I'm sorry about change; most of the time it happens so gradually we are not aware until we sneak a backward look. I'm glad the days I was poor are past and have not desire in the world to recall them. No do I wish poverty on anyone else.

Sunday is a beautiful day and a few golden leaves are blowing across the yards. My neighbor's house is empty now. She died two years ago, but I remember when I believed our time together was endless.

It was one of those periods in my life when we exchanged recipes and gossip, talked about religion and worried about our children. I still have her cookbook with the recipe for "easy make chocolate fudge," which I forgot to return and now it's too late, so I keep it as a memory.

There were the years when I thought wearing maternity clothes would last forever. Now, I find I am at the awkward age, too old to be a radiant mother and too young for hot flashes. Unfortunately this won't last forever either.

When we were young parents our Sunday ride was a visit to our parents. Now we stay at home awaiting visits from married children and their young.

Looking back each day seems part of a bright mosaic which I do not want to change or even bring back. Things happen...they are there forever. Somebody once said that life was not meant just to be lived, but celebrated.

Sometimes life can't be celebrated. Some days we are lucky to just survive. But it should be cherished, in us and in others. The changes only form the pattern; we weave the design, each minute, each day.

Chapter 1: Growing up Betty

I Grew Up in a Disaster Area

How many of you grew up in the same ominous climate, wondering how you survived so well; indeed, how you survived at all.

Over the heads of our young hangs the threat of wars, economic disaster, global warming and heaven knows what else... Over our own young heads in the peaceful 1930s hung threats, while not widely publicized, no less terrifying.

We were never allowed to leave the house without clean underwear. This was not so we would be nice to be near, or that cleanliness is next to Godliness, which they also thought, but didn't much of. We had to wear clean panties, so if we were hit by a car and killed the family wouldn't be disgraced.

I had one recurring nightmare of getting hit by a car and sitting up in Heaven watching my poor family leave town because I had died wearing socks with holes in them, even if they didn't show over my shoes. The undertaker would know, warned my folks.

My grandmother had this big thing about cleaning up the house before she went to bed. Naturally it wouldn't be for something pleasant, like waking up to a neat house.

"This is just in case anybody dies in the middle of the night and we have a lot of people coming in," she'd say, bustling around, plumping pillows and washing up the snackers' dishes. Who did she expect the lucky party to be, since we all looked fairly healthy at 10 p.m.?

"You never know," she'd warn, the voice of gloom. "You just never know." Naturally I hoped it wouldn't be me.

Rain gave you colds; drafts could bring on pneumonia; wearing tennis shoes could hurt your eyes. Never eat cherries and milk at the same meal, they'd warn, telling monstrous stories of relatives who died in agony from doing these things.

Never mention good fortune, because God might notice you were having a run of luck, and take it away from you. They never noticed that, being the Almighty, he was already aware of how we were faring.

Women didn't can during pregnancy because this was supposed to spoil the fruit and vegetables. Admittedly, I could ruin a nice comfortable confinement. Maybe this was how the thing got started. Neither did they put their hands in the dish water at certain times of the month.

Those were terrifying times for sure. Small wonder we didn't worry about poverty, racism and war. We had all we could do to just make it through the day and stay alive. These were the good old days your folks keep telling you about kids.

First Betsy Wetsy

Did I ever tell you about how I was really the one who invented the Betsy Wetsy Doll? I hope not. If I did, I am about to tell you again because I saw a little girl feeding one the other day.

Now dolls can grow hair, and shorten it again without even getting a haircut. They can talk, roller skate, play records and help you with your spelling. When I was a little girl all dolls did was lie around.

We had cradles, doll clothes and toy dishes, but the dolls were strictly non-participatory, although we loved them anyway. But I used to think it would be nice if I could give one of them a bottle once in a while and change something beside a dry diaper.

This was of course, before I got married and found that bottles and diapers were not games but a way of life. It reminds me of the time I saw the movie where Shirley Temple sang a song called, "When I Grow Up." In it was a line about, "I will have real dollies too, like the woman in the shoe."

How was I to know that Shirley, in addition to being America's Little Sweetheart, was also a prophetess? Anyway, if I had known about "real dollies' then, I would never have invented a doll that wet its pants.

But I did. My invention was a simple one. I found a small celluloid doll among my collection and poked a hole in its mouth large enough to fit the rubber nipple of my doll bottle. Hitherto, I had only been able to fake it.

Next, I poked a hole in the nipple so the milk would run through. I wasn't entirely unfamiliar with "real dollies," mind you, having a couple of baby brothers and sisters.

All right, so now, I had a doll filled to the brim with milk and no place for the milk to go so I could feed it over again. I have often

18

wondered if this was how the Creator went about things when he was putting people and creatures together piece by piece.

There was nothing to do but to put a drain system in my doll, which I did with the aid of a pin, and sure enough, the doll emptied out in no time at all.

But you must remember one thing; I grew up in a day and age when children were not even supposed to admit that this end of their anatomy existed. And here I was not only with my own, but one for my doll as well.

I didn't know much about anatomy, but I sure knew a heck of a lot about sin and hell fire and damnation, being a preacher's granddaughter, and for a day or two I was sure that God was going to hit me with lightening or something.

After a while it occurred to me that God didn't really care that I had invented a wetting doll. But there was the problem of hiding it from my mother who would have had a fit, or so I thought at the time.

It wasn't until years later that I realized that great inventors who grow rich don't go around wondering if God will hit them with lightening for having a bright idea.

Major decision: 'ready' for bra?

It may or may not have been for the good, but when I was a child (you'll never believe this kids) parents decided what kids wore. In fact, they even had a hand in such weighty matters as when a girl could wear lipstick or when a kid should or should not cut his hair.

There was the matter, considered then to be on par with the Jewish boy's Bar Mitzvah, of when one's daughter was "ready" to wear a bra. In those days they were called brassieres (pronounced brah-zeers). It required a summit conference of all the female members of the family: mother, grandmother, aunts.

Guidelines for the bra had nothing to do with bust measurements, incidentally. An amply bosomed 12-year-old was out of luck, bra-wise, if her female relatives didn't think age 12 was ready enough.

Rather, bra readiness was determined by the family's attitude toward maturity. When was girl old enough? When was she ready, strong enough to handle with virtue and prudence all of the responsibility that wearing a bra for the first time was supposed to require?

My mother who was a writer, my grandmother who was a minister's wife, and my aunt who was a minister, considered themselves quite liberal in their decision, that at age 13, I was ready. How they determined this I do not know, since until I was married I had trouble finding bras small enough. How many modern 13-year-olds have a size 29 bosom?

They dug in their heels about the lipstick and the silk stockings, however. Mother thought lipstick made me look too old. Grandmother said I would look 'hard' and Aunt Mable said the boys would think I was "fast." I was skinny, popeyed and homely, and no one at school ever thought I was "fast."

Being fast meant the boys hung around you like moths around a candle. I would have given anything to be fast. For a while, I put lipstick on before I got to school, but the boys still didn't think I was too quick. Eventually I decided there was more to being fast than wearing lipstick.

Silk stockings came a year later with family permission. But only for special occasions like Easter Sunday or a family wake. Today…the big question is, "When do I start shaving my legs?" And I tell my growing daughters, "When you think they look hairy."

Heaven knows what my mother and grandmother and Aunt Mabel would have decided.

Recalling the golden days in front of the radio

When I was a little kid the family radio reigned where the family television now sits -- in the living room. The difference was we only had to listen, leaving our eyes free to look out the window or read books.

The rule for me was no Buck Rogers in the 25th century -- my favorite radio show of all time -- unless after-school chores were finished. Things have not changed, only the people are new.

But a generation and a half of people raised in front of television sets might be surprised to know how family radios once dominated the household.

At 6 years old, I had already fallen under the advertising man's cereal spell. The spell casters were a pair of radio talk show hosts, Jolly Bill and Jane. Jolly Bill was a jolly man and Jane was a little girl. At least she talked like a little girl -- on radio you could never be sure. Anyway, their favorite cereal was Cream of Wheat, also making it mine.

Every morning I gobbled my Cream of Wheat while a presumably black character named Rastus told me and Jolly Bill and Jane how delicious and healthful it was. Rastus couldn't possibly appear in a modern day commercial, and it is a good thing. I couldn't stand Rastus.

He yucked when he laughed, which was often and loud, and said "Yowsah, yowsah boss," to Jolly Bill and "Lawsy Miss Jane," to Jane along with other stereotype lines. I found him an altogether irritating addition to the show and rejoiced when he yucked his way into silence. I didn't even know he was supposed to be "a colored man" until I saw his picture on a Cream of Wheat box one day.

He didn't at all resemble my little black friend who lived with her parents next door to me. They never yucked or said "yowsah." My friend and I played "movie star" together and mutually decided we'd be Clara Bow when we grew up -- unless we decided to be nurses or something else.

In the evening our world came to a complete stop so grownups all over America could listen to Lowell Thomas telling them the world news. At 7 they joined the rest of the country listening to Amos and Andy. I don't think a television show has been produced yet which produced the mass hypnosis generated each evening for 15 minutes by the adventures of these two.

If the communists had really wanted to take over the country they could have done so in the 30s any old evening between 7 and 7:15, and no American with a radio in the house would have noticed. On Sundays the grownups listened to the ravings of a hell-raising political priest by the name of Father Charles Coughlin.

Coughlin hated Jews and practically everyone else. On Sunday nights he came on the air to preach hate, doom, gloom, guilt and destruction. My father hated Coughlin. Every Sunday night he'd turn on the radio and make us all shut up so he could sit there and mutter and hate Coughlin. The priest's weekly tirades came to us from a Royal Oak church rather inappropriately called Shrine of the Little Flower.

When I grew up and knew more about theology, I wondered how he and the Little Flower (St. Theresa) ever got together even as pastor and church, and what they could possibly find to say to each other when they met in the hereafter. I suspected the difference in their approaches to life even at age 7 or 8, which was about the time he was tearing up the air waves.

Even know I wonder why the hierarchy of the Catholic Church of that day was so slow in telling Coughlin to shut up and sit down because he was giving Christianity a bad name. Organized religions always seem slow noticing demagogues in their midst. But I digress.

Along the years of my growing up I collected a whole string of favorite shows, Jack Armstrong, Orphan Annie, the Lone Ranger, the Shadow and of course the king, Buck Rogers.

Staying home from school was a treat because early soaps (which lasted only 15 minutes each) ran all day -- a perfect smorgasbord of heart-rending adventure. My favorite then was the Romance of Helen Trent who "discovered romance in life didn't end at 35." I'll admit I wondered sometimes how an old lady of 35 found love even on the radio.

This isn't a longing for the "good old days," because there isn't such a thing. It is only so you will know they were there next time someone kids you about your addiction to some really dumb television show. You are your parents' child, remember.

Gym class wasn't that much fun

When John was born I shared a room with a former Olympic speed skater who'd given birth to a 5-pound son in approximately 15 minutes. The way the hospital staff ran around congratulating her, you'd have thought she won a gold medal in childbirth. Nine-pound John Christopher Hansen was a tot on a different scale.

There had been no need for me to hurry to the hospital. We could have driven to a hospital in Omaha and still had plenty of time for me to deliver this child we used to call, "Huey the Baby Giant."

For five days she and the nurses managed to make me feel as if I had somehow flunked childbirth. Healthy Hannah skipped around the maternity ward, flexing her skating muscles while I sacked out exhausted from having produced almost twice what she'd produced.

And there was the indignity. Healthy Hannah, whose real name escapes me, thankfully, looked so much healthier than I did; the nurses assumed the strapping infant belonged to her. They kept handing me the puny one.

Anyway, John grew up to be a star athlete, who could say "football" before he could say "mama." He almost reinforced the maternity nurses' obvious belief that someone had switched babies. If he hadn't looked just like me, I'd have wondered too. No one in our family has ever been athletically inclined.

Notice that little girl in the commercials who is the emotional pits because she's the last chosen for dodgeball? Do you know what it's like to be chosen last for everything? Do you know how a self-image suffers when the teacher makes someone put you on their team?

My aversion to athletics is more than genetic. It's the result of a traumatic experience with gym suffered when I first encountered the awful subject in junior high school.

My gym teacher looked as if she could be a Marine drill sergeant in drag, and I was never sure she wasn't. She regarded me, not only as unfit, but as stupid. Had a gas chamber been an alternative to an "E" in gym, she'd have sent me there to avoid weakening the race.

There was an escape from the thrice-weekly hell, but we girls could only try it every 28 days. You tiptoed up to the gym teacher and whispered, so no one else could hear, "M." She'd nod sympathetically and cross off a blessed five days. This meant that for a week you could read in the bleachers.

My problem came when I lost count and whispered the magic letter every 21 days, then every other week. The teacher tried to save me. How, she wondered could anyone NOT like to get elbowed in the liver in a basketball game, or kicked in the head during calisthenics? What would become of me with such a poor attitude?

At the end of the year she handed me my "E" in gym with the comment that I'd probably have awfully puny children.

I was always sorry I couldn't show her John the football, basketball, tennis player who said "football" before he said "mama." Maybe he had a point.

Oh, to be a kid again, and have your own secret places

The world of children is filled with secret places. Only children can see them, only they can lead you there.

They made these secret places and breathed life into the phantom folks who inhabit them. Few, if any, grown-ups are ever invited in.

The secret places of my own childhood came to mind a few days ago, watching a couple of youngsters turn the dark space behind the living room sofa into a mountain hideaway. To the grown-ups in the living room it was, of course, still a sofa.

Over the years we lose the eerie ability of children to create unseen worlds out of the most ordinary of objects. Our grown-up conversations must be woven of sturdy, sensible material stretched between two solid and live individuals. No adults ever talk with make-believe friends.

I couldn't have been more than 8 years old -- a child of parents who believed certain amount of time spent daily in the fresh air was healthy for little people. As a little person, I failed to see anything healthy about being bundled into scarves and boots and shoved into a chilly fall Saturday afternoon made for daydreaming indoors.

But underneath a thick tangle of shrubbery, in a corner formed by the front porch and the house, I discovered a place for a little town. Maybe I was inspired by thousands of little sticks that had fallen from the horse chestnut tree to cover the wet sidewalk on a dark, rainy October day. Maybe the tiny patch of sheltered ground asked me to build a town.

It took a while to gather the little sticks and form them into curbs for streets and squares for houses. The sticks refused to stack up like logs to make real walls, so I contented myself with shortening some of them so the imaginary walls at least had pretend doors.

For a long time I played in this imaginary town, visiting with the pleasant townsfolk who moved in as soon as they noticed a village had sprung up in this secret place. But they disappeared forever, like Brigadoon, the moment I went in the house to eat supper. An evening storm arose while I was eating and blew away the ruins.

Best of all were the times when I could be a princess. When I was a very little girl, influenced by fairy tale books, I was positive I was really a princess.

Looking back at my childhood, I now realize this sometimes made things very difficult for my family and friends. Princesses can be very difficult.

Once my throne room was the foyer of a friend's house. A high-back chair, very throne-like, sat in the curve of a staircase at the top of which was a jewel-colored stained glass window. But I didn't stay long because my friend interrupted my royal dreams with suggestions we go outdoors and play cowboys with the boys.

Another, better palace sprang up from a tangled clump of trees and roots on a little rise of land overlooking Lake Michigan.

Seated on a jeweled throne, which grown-up strollers on the beach saw merely as a little space between two birch trees, I watched for ships to return from distant lands filled with emerald crowns and white velvet robes.

Behind me, my kingdom flourished in a dazzling landscape of sand dunes. While I dreamed my princess dreams, a city of royal people went about their daily activities, departing at sunset without leaving a single footprint on the pale and shifting hills where I had brought them to life.

But you need not be a solitary child to create a secret place. My friends and I could change a single cherry tree in an average back yard into a rain forest filled with savages and wild beasts.

We built trains from bikes and toy wagons, transformed sandboxes into cities and forts and made nurseries out baby dolls under desks and tables.

That was a long time ago. So when do humans lose the ability to make magic? I sometimes suspect their magic is lost soon after it is discovered by parents who, fearing such awful power in the hands of the innocent, convince them it is nonsense.

A tree is just a tree, nothing more. Castles do not rise on sand dunes and disappear without a trace. And you, my child, are not a princess. Turn your back on all of these daydreams before they swallow you up forever. Only the grown-up truths are real.

Like fairies, magic dies when children, their heads confused by arguments against it, agree to forget.

Somewhere along the way I was forced to concede that I wasn't really a princess. But one time I did build a little secret place under the bushes by our front porch. And one time I sat in a palace by the sea and wore an emerald crown. That was a long time ago.

Getting organized: It's on my list somewhere

Among my list of speaking engagements for the coming year is one where my assigned topic is "on getting organized." The invitation requested an informative talk but added, "feel free to inject some humor into it."

The humor has already been injected, according to some of my friends, by the mere fact that I was selected to talk on how to be organized. But they scoff unjustly. I may forget where I put my purse occasionally or daydream on the way to work and drive somewhere else. But beneath this absent-minded exterior is a machine of organization.

My secret? I'm a list maker. My mother was a list maker before me and her mother. I have several kids whose second act in the morning after going to the bathroom and snarling at everyone is to make a list of what else they plan to do that day. If all of the lists in our family were stretched end to end they could be completed at the other end by someone in Australia.

But face it. A neatly written list of the day's tasks is impressive. The writer is impressed. After all, a list has a way of leaving the maker feel as if at least one thing is already accomplished - the list. Other people are impressed. A list of tasks gives off the message of organization, efficiency and control.

A list with a majority of the items checked or crossed off tells the reader by chance that the list maker does not take his or her list lightly. After all, anyone can sit down in the morning and list everything that is supposed to happen that day. To actually accomplish the designated projects requires real dedication.

A hint from an expert list maker: If you don't intend to do any of the listed tasks, at least have the good sense not to leave your list lying around for the prying eyes of others. Or be really dishonest and check off a job or two just to make your list look good to passers-by who like to stop and observe the contents of your desk as they chat.

You, who never list and say you envy us listers for our efficiency and command of our lives, might be less envious if you know the truth. The truth is nobody who is really organized and efficient needs a list. The truly organized person has no need to itemize their appointed rounds on paper. They have an inborn mental list that came with their genes.

My genes were unlisted in heaven evidently, which is why, for most of my life I have had to supply my own. If listing were not a genetic factor, I too would be running around mentally ticking off my days, one, two, three and son on. But anyone can adjust to a lack in their lives.

We unlisted individuals have profited by the invention of such things as little lined notepads that fit a corner of the desk or nestle in a purse pocket. At one time making a list was extremely difficult when lists had to be chiseled on stone tablets. No doubt there were some souls who spent a lifetime chiseling their lists on granite only to grow old and feeble before they could chisel the checkmarks on them.

On my desk at this very moment is a list. Anyone who cares to look at it will know that today I have several phone calls to make, a column to finish and some interviews to set up. They will see that in addition to all of these work tasks, there are groceries to be bought and errands to be run on the way home. Basically, it looks like I've got a heck of a lot to do. How will I ever get through it all? I won't.

Tomorrow I will revise the list, removing what was done today and adding new jobs that came up overnight. The list has no end and won't be finished until I am. But I have the satisfaction of knowing when I face my Maker and He asks me to review my life I won't have to do any soul searching. I'll just get out my list. It's all there, the done and the undone.

I just hope I can find it when the time arrives. List makers sometimes get disorganized and lose their lists. They come apart at the seams for a day or so, but that's another column

Chicken Little Syndrome

I have this hereditary disease I call Chicken Little Syndrome. I know it's inherited because I remember my mother and grandmother suffering periodic attacks of "The Sky is Falling." At this time, I never dreamt that I, too, carried that same genetic defect. It came on me gradually as I grew up.

Do I hear a sneeze? Somebody is catching pneumonia and we must begin immediately to make funeral plans. If it is our own sneeze, we should let our loved ones know what we plan to wear to the funeral and what we'd like said about us at it.

A headache presages a brain tumor. Nobody calls long distance just to talk, AT&T notwithstanding. Every cloud hides a silver tornado and there's a stock market crash looming around every corner.

"It's a funny sort of day," my mother would note ominously, watching thunderheads gather on an August afternoon. Nothing unusual for this time of year in Michigan. But we just knew mother was hoping against hope she would be able to say after the disastrous windstorm, "I just said to the kids, it was a strange sort of day and I was right."

I remember the day my mother thought my little brother had infantile paralysis. This was what they called polio before the discovery of the Salk vaccine. It was a dreaded disease. My brother came limping downstairs on that fateful morning.

"He's got infantile paralysis," shrieked my mother. All morning long she kept him on the sofa, feeling his forehead, refusing to hear his protests that he was feeling fine. Only during a trip to the bathroom did mother discover he had put both legs into the same pant-leg opening of his underwear.

"Well, he could have had infantile paralysis," insisted my mother. "It just goes to show you can't be too careful," she added, ignoring the fact that her son was in perfect health.

My sister says she also has Chicken Little Syndrome and described the awful morning she was dressing for work and her ring refused to slip over her knuckle. "Good heavens," she thought, "I've got arthritis and this is the first symptom. I won't be able to type and I'll lose my job and - there go the car payments. I'm doomed to a life with crippled fingers."

A moment later, returning to her jewelry box, she noticed another, smaller ring had slipped inside it and stuck. But you can never tell. Any moment she might get arthritis again.

Chicken Little Syndrome isn't confined to worry over disease and weather. Some of my aunts and uncles lived through the Great Depression and now await its return with all of the preparatory zeal of those who spend their lives getting ready for the end of the world.

"What if there is another depression and HE is laid off?" asked these prophets of doom each time a child of theirs bought something on credit. The offending spenders, being warned, would hurry up and pay their debts before they caused a Great Depression and their folks would say, "We told you so."

The election of a Republican president never failed to set off an acute attack of Chicken Little Syndrome in that branch of the family. It mattered little how peaceful or prosperous we might be during these administrations. They never forgot what happened when their parents voted for Herbert Hoover.

Some Chicken Little attacks disappear with old age. The times when I had named the baby, changed the layette and repainted the nursery, all in the space of a week, only to discover, thank heaven, wrong again.

Those of us who suffer from the syndrome seldom find life uneventful. If there isn't an impending disaster around, we will think one up quicker than you can say, "The sky is falling!

Plumb lines for wood-be handyperson

This is the story of how I came to know and love that most male of hangouts – the hardware store. Who cares about integrating restrooms? Truly equality arrives when a woman can walk into a hardware store and ask for a female (or male) plug without a quaver or a giggle.

As Orwell said, all are created equal, but some are more equal than others. Those of us women who are most equal can find our way to proper-size nails and bolts with the authority of an experienced handyperson.

I believe I really arrived in this man's world the day I was able to ask for a stud-finder in a hardware store and not laugh or look away when I asked. The secret, I decided after wandering around trying to find one without asking for it, is to look the male clerk straight in the eye with an expression that says, "I'll kill the first stupid so-and-so who cracks a smile."

A stud-finder, for readers who have never needed one, is a magnetized device to help you find a sturdy place on the wall to hang your plants so they don't come crashing down on your head. A stud-finder seeker is what I was before I got up the courage to ask for one.

After I'd found it, I also discovered molly bolts which screw into a wall or ceiling anyplace and eliminate having to find a stud unless your hanging plant weighs 500 pounds or so.

And you'll never believe the identity of the eager guides into this fascinating world of hardware; its men themselves. Ask a man you trust – your father, lover, husband, friend, son, good buddy. Tell him you're planning to replace the washers on your bathroom faucets, or whatever project you've got going.

Ask for the exact size, shape, brand, whatever, even stock numbers if the item requires it. Then go forth into hardware country to buy your washers, bolts and screws.

There's another approach you might try. It sounds a trifle like "helpless little female me," until you realize the large percentage of men can't tell a level from a plane either. That's the "I want to start this project, but I don't know what I'll need in the way of tools and supplies.

It's been my experience that hardware salesmen are in their glory with an assignment like this and surprisingly honest about not selling you overly expensive tools, and in offering other hints on how to keep expenses down. They often have printed directions or manuals in the stores.

I'll never forget my first crash course in wallpapering when I decided last year to decorate the bathroom. I came home from the hardware store, not only with supplies but with a couple of pages of handwritten notes covering everything from sizing the walls to keeping ceiling paper from falling down as you pasted it up.

Don't hurry when you get to the hardware store. There's too much to see and learn about. Neatly stacked on shelves, hanging on racks or piled into bins are everything you will ever need to keep your place fixed up or to build a new one, if that's your idea of a project.

Just the other day I was browsing in a hardware department of a large local store. I found a stapling gun and a drill that just fit my hand in size and weight. I picked up a roll of duct tape to mend my dryer vent and found some screws in a size I'd been looking for to replace in a lamp.

I appreciate hardware stores. Now I know why men can hardly wait to get there on Saturday mornings. Neither can I.

Capricorn horoscopes get my goat!

For years I've been a fan of numerous horoscope columns and followed them religiously, in a manner of speaking. My one hope, as my eye catches the one for this month, week or day, is that sooner or later one of them will tell me something I'm glad to read.

The problem is I was born a Capricorn. As we all know, Capricorns are considered to be the wet blankets of the zodiac before whom all laughter ceases and orders are immediately called off.

It does my frivolous heart no good to read that I am sober, hard-working, plodding, practical and responsible. How many fun people do you know who willingly hand around with sober, hard-working responsible duds, unless they happen to be other Capricorns.

All work and no play makes Jack a Capricorn and Jill's image is even words. Our horoscopes tell us to laugh a little more, to relax, take it easy and not work so hard. The rest of you non-Caps have no idea how hard it is to relax and have fun when you're being told what a drudge you really are.

I'm not arguing. Astrologers know what they're talking about. I believe everything they say. I just hate to believe they are saying it's about me, that's all. My Scorpio sister is "sexy." My Gemini brother is a "sparkler," and my Leo best friend a "leader."

My astrological character reference reads like a cross between the Boy Scout Oath and the Sermon on the Mount, hardly an invitation to an evening of scarlet sin.

I grew up with a whole family of people from other signs in the zodiac. Not one of them even suspected that among them dwelt a pillar of the zodiac. They thought I was the family scatterbrain and no one told them differently.

But that was before horoscopes were as popular as they are now. It's too bad. That was a time in my life when I would have appreciated a good run-down on what Capricorns are really supposed to be like. They, my family, would have been surprised, to say the least.

A few incidents may have led them astray. There was the day the pillar of the zodiac, at home alone, accidentally locked the meter man in the basement, forgot he was down there and went away. There were all of those other days when the industrious, hard-working Capricorn snuck out of the house leaving them with the chores.

As far as the overworked Leo and Scorpio back home were concerned, I hardly qualified as a drudge. Crazy, maybe, drudgy, never.

But hope springs like rising signs to those of us who daily read out forecasts. If I have one Capricorn quality to my name, it is persistence. I keep coming back, reading my own dull little segment, knowing if I do this long enough and often enough, some astrology writer will relent and tell me that today I am sexy, clever, witty and irresistible.

One of these days the Scorpios, Leos, Pisces, and Geminis will be forced to shoulder the burden of responsibility then they'll know what it's been like for us Capricorns all of these centuries.

They will know, if they don't already, that nobody else in the zodiac would have had the patience to go around all their lives being so stuffy and well, upstanding--unless, possibly, Virgos.

I am convinced that when astrologers assigned all of these tough stuff to the Capricorns, it was because the Capricorns were at another meeting someplace and, not being present to defend themselves, got stuck with it.

What I keep hoping is that one of these days they'll find out Saturn was a million miles out of line and astrologers have been wrong about Capricorns all along. We are too cute, funny, mysterious and desirable. People do want us at their parties for our wit and charm, and the orgy doesn't even start until we get there.

The discovery of this error can't come too soon for me. It's been lonely for us goats up here on the mountain top watching the rest of you have all the fun.

Chapter 2: All in the Family

Civil war breaks out at Old House

When our family was young and we went out for an evening we left them in charge of a teenage baby sitter until the fateful morning Stevie reported at breakfast that his big brother and the baby sitter "kiss each other on the lips when you are away."

We knew he'd finally reached the awkward age…too young to be left alone and too old to be trusted with a baby sitter. Next we hired an elderly, no-nonsense lady who charged a quarter more an hour but our peace of mind when we left the children made it worth the money.

Then we discovered we no longer needed a sitter. We could leave the older children in charge of the younger ones. It seemed that we were free at last until we discovered that brothers and sisters left without their parents for more than 10 minutes tend to kill each other.

What's more the longer parents stay away the worse the mayhem gets. And it's no use trying to hire the elderly no-nonsense lady who charges a quarter more an hour. She refuses to come back here anymore.

Nothing ties nervous parents up in further nervous knots so much as going out for an evening on the town, coming home happy and relaxed for the first time in a month only to find that civil war has broken out in their happy home.

"He was beating on me all the time you were gone," yells the first one out to the car. He's the first one because he stood waiting for you on the corner and chased you for a block. "I wasn't beating on that lyin' little punk. He was throwing stuff all over the house and I just trapped him a little." This is the second kid to reach the car.

"Everybody was bad as heck," reports the oldest as you walk into the ruins, "Yeah, I noticed," you reply grimly picking your way through the wreckage.

"Well, thank heaven the outer walls are still standing," says their father.

It is a house divided as well as broken. It's the good guys against the bad guys depending upon who has the floor.

"Let's hear both sides of the story," say the parents in an all-out attempt at impartiality. Have you ever listened to a battle saga in which both sides emerged as black hearted villains? You have if you are parents who have gone out for the evening and left the older children to babysit the younger ones and then come home to find the house under siege.

Well we started out trying to be impartial so we might as well go all the way. The next thing to do is throw out all arguments as invalid, spank everyone in the house under the age of 14 and then make them clean up the place while the parents sit and enjoy a cold drink and a chat.

It's about as mean as parents can get but it clears the air.

Naming the Baby

Having named nine babies, I've come to believe it's one of the most important jobs parents will ever do, after giving birth of course. Whether or not the wrong name will scar a person for life is debatable, but you can't be too careful. Baby naming has its pitfalls and mistakes. This why choosing a name for your child taken quite seriously throughout all of history. You don't even have to be a future king to encounter trouble. Biblical history is full of baby naming stories.

A few Sundays ago we Catholics celebrated the birthday of St. John the Baptist. As the Gospel was read, I wondered if biblical history would have changed had Elizabeth and John's father had caved to the objections of everyone they knew who insisted they name their baby "Zechariah," after his dad. Friends, relatives, neighbors, and passers-by I suppose all with suggestions. The naysayers offered no logical reason (naysayers rarely have any) other than no one in their family ever named a child John before.

It is possible Elizabeth and Zechariah might have given in to all that pressure had God not intervened, for reasons known only to God. Elizabeth seemed to have made up her mind right away. "John!" Zechariah appeared to have second thoughts. God then rendered him speechless, so he was forced to write the name 'John" on a piece of parchment before he could talk again.

I wanted to name my fourth son "Christopher Robin," a little boy immortalized in stories and poems by his father, English writer A.A. Milne. They were very popular at the time. I read them to my own small sons; tales of an adorable child with a bear companion, just about his size named Pooh.

But, like Elizabeth and Zechariah, when it came to naming the baby, his father and I found ourselves overwhelmed with unwanted opinions and suggestions from practically everyone we knew, beginning with my mother-in-law. She was firm in her belief that all babies needed to be named after dead relatives —her dead relatives that is. My dead relatives didn't count.

"So, who are you naming him for?" she asked. She pointed out that the William and Robert were already taken, but Andrew was still open for the honor. Andrew was her father-in-law's name. Dead of course; had been for years. Never knew him. My own family was no better. Dad's side favored names like Ebenezer and Abel, dead relatives from my Grandfather Morningstar's dead or alive. Mother offered names reflecting her New England heritage, like Lyman, Justus, Ralph or Henry. Also, being Catholic we had to stick a saint's name in there for baptism.

My first choice, "Christopher Robin" was met with blank stares by those who'd never heard of A.A. Milne, and sarcastic question is like "Where did you get an outlandish name like that?" Or, "A character out of a kid's book? Are you nuts?" Daddy, whose oldest son was named after him and second son after my father, allowed me first choice on this one and withheld comment if he even had one, which I doubt or he would have said.

Unlike Elizabeth and Zechariah, God did not intervene to save our son from "that name. But an older, wiser human did. Taking me aside he pointed out that while "Christopher Robin" was indeed a very cute name, the original CR was only six-years old. Cute is fine when one is six. But a name like that could cause real problems for a grown-up man, hoping to be taken seriously in the adult world, particularly one looking for a responsible job.

Then of course there was the church. At the time Catholics were required to baptize babies with the names of saints which accounted for future many generations of Mary's, Josephs, Catherine's and Michaels. Christopher was presumed to be a saint in 1950. St. Robin? I don't think so.

I envy today's parents. They aren't so influenced by opinions of friends, relatives or religion. Heedless of others' advice, they turn other sources; characters from novels, movies or television shows, maybe rock stars. Girls get named Madison or the mom's birth name if it's a good solid Anglo Saxon surnames. Peperovitz, or names ending in "wicz," are avoided.

The original Christopher Robin, made famous by his father was teased by other boys as a teenager. For years he resented his father having prospered exploiting his childhood. Years later his mother sold his father's manuscripts before she died and it was years after that before he collected royalties from the Disney version of his life. Adding insult to injury, 21st Century Disney educated, if they think of Christopher Robin at all, it's as a straight man" for the wit and wisdom of the Disney movie for its chosen star, Winnie the Pooh.

So be careful when you name the baby. Perhaps if you listen to the baby before it is born, he or she may whisper the exact, just right name. But don't count on it. If the daddy agrees and the rest of the world shuts up, it'll be fine. In the case of the son about whom I write, I reluctantly agreed with my dad; "Christopher Robin" was definitely not a name a future employer could see or hear without laughing. Like Elizabeth and Zechariah, we named him John.

Life without him joyless

John celebrated his birthday by making 20 points in the basketball game. Later his teammates shared a pizza trimmed with 17 candles.

If God had shown us every 17-year-old boy who had ever lived and asked us to choose the one we wanted it would have been John at first sight. "I like people, school, sports, food and parties," exuberantly reads his high school autobiography. You can believe it. His days are filled with activity, studying, eating, working, playing and visiting with his friends.

John is fun. When you talk to him he talks back. If there is something going on from Youth Council like putting up chairs in the gym he wants to be there. When he isn't practicing some sport he is reading about football, basketball, golf, baseball or bridge, you name it and he'll try it, even if he isn't very good at it.

John has a tender and compassionate heart. He was sponsor for his retarded brother's confirmation last spring. When we drove home from Lapeer State Home he was not too "cool" to share the tears we shed.

If we had not had him we wouldn't have really known what we had missed. And we might not have had him. I had been quite ill with a serious thyroid condition and another baby was just out of the question. But I was pregnant.

Since no one had the temerity to suggest that he be destroyed as a mere seedling because of this, we braved it through, and he was born on schedule; strong, healthy and alert to life even when just a few minutes old.

I myself was completely well in a matter of weeks, and John was followed by five more children. But what if John had been killed while still in his mother's womb? Would we, now and then, catch ourselves wondering what kind of child this might have been? And would we ever have imagined a boy like John?

Life without him would be somewhat less of a joy than it is; less filled with fun and affection and hope for the future. But John is alive, today was his birthday and we had a cake, a special red cake he always wanted on his birthday. Maybe he likes it for its many fabulous names, Red Velvet Cake, Red Carpet and $200 Red Cake, which appeal to his sense of the dramatic. Or maybe it's because red is a symbol of life and John is glad to be alive. The flame from 17 candles gives a splendid light in a home where there is a boy like John.

A beautiful spring day

"And He laid His hand upon them, and they were filled with the Holy Spirit."

It was beautiful on the day 450 Catholic retarded children assembled at Lapeer State Home and Training School to receive the Sacrament of Confirmation. Bishop Breitenbeck of the Archdiocese of Detroit confirmed patients in the gymnasium of the Woodside School at the home. He was assisted by seminarians and by sisters from Marygrove College who teach catechism at the institution.

The "children," who range in age from early teens to 60, sat in the gym with their sponsors behind them and the bishop came to each in turn. Parents and relatives sat in the bleachers watching the simple, ancient ceremony which was first recorded in the Acts of the Apostles. Later Bishop Breitenbeck visited some of the cottages where he confirmed those too severely afflicted to leave the buildings in which they live.

Afterward there was a chance for families to visit with their children and with each other. We smile, but do not look too closely, because it is an intrusion, it seems, to stumble upon the pain and the question which is always present in the eyes of the parents. For each of these retarded children had once lain in the body of his mother, the secret hope of future generations. And now the hope is gone, but in its place is the strength and wisdom which comes from knowing that perfection is never required by those who truly love.

It is said that when the early Christians were being led to death that one Roman citizen remarked, "See how they love each other." And I think that if the children of Lapeer have any lesson at all for us, it is that all of us are creatures of weakness and fault and maybe we should care for others because of this and not in spite of it.

Truly this is our Father's world and each of us has a right to be here. So whether a person is marred in mind, body or spirit does not matter. His right to the concern and respect of his fellow men is the same.

After a while it was time to say goodbye and the families who had come to witness the confirmation of their retarded children began walking quietly back to their cars in the bright spring sunshine. And was our gloom after all, "but the shadow of His hand outstretched caressingly?" A sudden spring breeze blew across the open fields and dried my tears as we walked along.

Buying a pagan baby

This is the story of Patricia and the Pagan Baby. It took place back in the dear days when guardian angels clustered on pink and blue clouds, watching over the Catholic school attended by my children. It many of the cold realities which, if acknowledged would have made raising a large family much harder.

"Five dollars will buy a pagan baby," Sister had announced to the first classes. The money would be raised for foreign missionaries. Five dollars would supply food, care and education for one of the unbaptized little pagans. We, her parents, knew this. Patricia, at age six, did not. So it was with much joyful anticipation that she announced her intention to save up five dollars to buy her own pagan baby.

They've got lots of them over in Africa and India," she told the family at dinner. "I don't care where it comes for. I don't even care if it's a boy or a girl," she concluded magnanimously. "And I'll take care of it myself too." She added, eyeing her four-year-old brother, two year-old sister and the infant on my lap. "That will be nice," I heard myself murmuring.

Saving five dollars at age six is comparable to an unemployed 19-

year-old trying to save $500. There were no aunts or godparents who lived nearby to stuff a dollar or two into her little bank. She gathered soda bottles and cashed them in at the corner grocery store and half her birthday monthly.

I can hardly wait until it gets here, she'd say adding another nickel to here savings. I know I should say something to her, but her happy anticipation and plans for her pagan baby was just too much. I wasn't even sure she would even have believed me. And with four little ones seventeen months apart, the last thing I'd ever want would be a pagan baby delivered to my door by mail.

The Christian deliveries were coming along almost faster than I could handle them.

Oh, I did try to explain a little, telling her that the sisters would send her money across the sea where other nuns would make sure the babe was fed and loved and cared for and even sent to school, and wouldn't that be lovely. She'd just stare at me for an instant and go back to planning for the arrival. The day she finally took her savings to school, I waited for her to come home, dreading the moment and wondering how I would comfort a tearful little girl.

What happened at school, I never found out. She was very matter of fact about the whole thing. "I found out they don't mail us the babies. That wouldn't be good to them and they would miss their mothers and be really sad. But the money will help them grow up and learn to be Catholic and go to heaven."

That was long ago. Now we know that St. Philomena never existed and St. Christopher wasn't going to save us from an auto accident if we dangled a little statue of him from our rear view mirrors, and that there was nothing wrong with eating meat on Friday.

But that nothing to do with this, other than I sometimes mourn that lost innocence, wrong though it was in many ways. And sometimes I wish I could have bought Patricia her pagan baby back when she was only six.

'Surly Riser' becomes 'Miss Sunshine'

Around home, I'm known as *The One Who Hates to Get Up*. We also have *Cheerful Awaker* (Himself, you might know), *Morning Sleepwalker*, and then we have *Surly Riser*.

Is there one of these in your house? I won't identify our own sunbeam other than to say that at the sound of her little footsteps on the stairs blood pressures rise, ulcers twinge and tension headaches tense.

"Gee, thanks a lot," she snarls. "I thought I said to get me up at 7:30. It's 7:31. Boy!"

Boy! But you tell yourself, as you've told yourself since the first day she ever got up, "Steady there. Maybe this time a soft answer will turneth away the wrath."

It doesn't turneth a doggone thing. "What's for breakfast?" she demands as she has every morning of her life. She knows the morning menu never varies. A choice of 19 different kinds of cold cereal, eggs, bacon, pancakes, rolls or toast.

"Ferget it," is the gloomy suggestion after you've again recited the meager menu.

"OK."

"OK? Sure it's OK to see your own child go starving to school."

"Well then, suppose you decide."

"I guess I might just as well have scrambled eggs, bacon, toast and pancakes since that's all you've got. Boy, what a crummy house."

After choking down her miserable meal Surly Riser gets ready for school. By now the whole family has turned surly including *Cheerful Awaker. The One Who Hates to Get Up* dashes around finding *Surly Riser's* missing textbook, pressing her blouse, smiling, soothing, watching the clock and wondering if it is going to stay 8 a.m. forever, while the *Surly Riser* paces the house looking for her shoes and accusing *The One Who Hates to Get Up* of deliberately disposing of them.

Maybe time has frozen, thinks *The One Who Hates to Get Up*. I'll be here for eternity hearing *Surly Riser* tell how her sister ruins her clothes. How long, oh Lord, how long?

Time has not frozen. It is 8:25 and *Surly Riser* stamps vengefully out the door. *The One Who Hates to Get Up* wonders who will be her first victim. It's like dumping a starving piranha into a bowl of innocent goldfish. Hoping vaguely for the best. *The One Who Hates to Get Up* wanders back to her bed.

It is PTA night. Unhappily *Surly Riser's* mother approaches the teacher. What will she say?

"We're so delighted with that *Little Miss Sunshine* of yours," burbles the teacher, "That happy smile. Truly it makes my day just seeing her walk in the room."

Mrs. Hates to Get Up has been hearing this since *Surly Riser* started kindergarten, and as long as she lives she will never figure out what happens between the time *Surly Riser* leaves home and the minute she walks smiling into her classroom. But she is mighty glad it happens.

Get out of my way! It's For Me!

Sports experts will often say about athletes that it isn't size that counts. Its speed and hustle that makes a champion…heart and all that. I think that the ones who say this a lot were too small to make the team in school and this makes them feel better.

Until Patricia became a freshman in high school I always disagreed. Size counted. But given a chance Patricia who is 5 feet tall and wears a petite size nine, could quarterback for the Baltimore Colts. Because when the phone rings, she can single handedly outflank the entire family including a couple of 6 foot older brothers.

"It's for me! It's for me!" she shrieks racing through the house, stiff arming her brothers and sisters, shouldering aside her parents and soaring over any furniture to her path. Oddly enough it usually is for her if it isn't for John. The rest of us rarely get a phone call.

When she reaches the house, after school she immediately phones the same girlfriend she walked home with. Then she pays her respects to her two sisters-in-law and her brother's girlfriend, filling them in on everything that happened since yesterday including what came in the mail.

Homework time she places the phone beside her on the kitchen table where it serves as a handy reference along with the dictionary and encyclopedia. I do not recall the boys becoming addicted to phones until they started going steady with girls. Then they carried the phone into the closet so we couldn't monitor their conversations. This was before wireless telephones. Instead we had a 24-foot telephone line, otherwise they restricted their phoning to occasional "What's today's history assignment?" and "Where'll I meet you?" calls outstanding for their terseness and lack of any evidence about what or to whom they were speaking. With their parents hanging around they clearly regarded phoning as pretty undercover stuff.

Once in a great while the call isn't for Patricia and there is always a small moment of triumph for the lucky one. Mostly we stand back or duck for cover when the phone rings, like the other evening. I didn't hear a thing. But, suddenly Patricia burst into the house, knocked over a chair and flattened the family. "It's for me!" she yelled and dove for the silent phone.

I picked myself off the floor. "I think you're hearing things," said her father. Her brother began picking up toppled furniture. "The window was open and a phone did ring. But it was next door," he grumbled. Patricia was not a bit crestfallen by this revelation.

"Well anyway when it does ring here it will be for me," she remarked and went out to ride the tandem bike. She had no sooner disappeared than the telephone did ring. It was for Patricia. None of us was surprised.

Weightlifters had nothing on Girl-child

I don't think the task of getting children off to school each day would be any big deal if it weren't for all of the stuff you have to send with them. I could be forgetful, but in my own memory of early school days I went skipping off every morning with a nickel for milk and an apple for the teacher.

Number One Girl-child stands out in my mind as an example of a child whose daily trip to school always looked like she was running away from home and taking everything with her. Her school needs weighed more than she did, but she faithfully dragged them back and forth every day.

Once I had a conversation with a friend who was worried over "the heavy load" her son was "carrying in college." To which I replied, "You think his load is heavy. You should see the junk Girl-child lugs to school and she's only in first grade."

Into her oversized book-bag went her workbooks, her flash cards, her lunch and her uniform sweater. Then we packed a drawstring bag with her gym shoes and her "show-and-tell" of the day. The latter was anything she could lift and drag out of the house which had not previously been exhibited at school. This was not easy.

Girl-child regarded show-and-tell as a required subject for graduation from elementary school. She often held up the morning packing while we rummaged through all of our belongings for something as yet, unknown.

Into odd corners of her bags and clothing we tucked the notes which daily traveled back and forth between school, in growing quantities. Discussing this with the parents of my grandchildren, I've come to the conclusion that there is a whole underground industry which gets paid for dreaming up forms to be sent home, filled out by parents and returned to school.

Girl-child attended in a parochial school which added to her daily load. You didn't need to be rich to go there. You did need to have a lot of spare change on hand. I recall it as a time of non-stop silver collection. The word of the day was "Come and bring money."

I sent money to school for missionaries, Chinese babies, presents for the basketball coach, nuns 90th birthdays, the Red Cross, Holy Childhood stamps, milk, hot lunch and the poor – a group I often thought of joining.

And of course there were the occasional collections to buy a pagan baby. This sounds both illegal and a heck of a brother. But I was coldly informed by the nun I said this to that the funds would be sent overseas to be used for the Christian training of unconverted infants.

I always supposed that as she grew older, Girl-child's load would lighten, but I supposed wrong. Her burden grew with her. I lived to see college paraphernalia coming back and forth each year in packing cases born to our door in trucks.

I don't think we ever forgot anything. If we had, somebody would have said something and they never did.

My Daughter, the Mechanic

The only time I ever notice anything wrong with my car is when it doesn't move. Then I am inclined to think that there is something wrong with it, or that perhaps it is stuck.

No so my daughter, the mechanic, without whom my driving would be infinitely more enjoyable and less threatening. Driving up main street, I am under the impression that all goes well with my automobile. It is moving, isn't it?

"Listen," says the longhaired, jean-clad beauty at my side. "Do you hear THAT?"

"What?"

"There's something wrong with your back left wheel. I heard it the other day. I think it may be going to come off any minute."

Its rush hour, traffic is bumper to bumper, there's a 40-foot truck looming in the next lane, and she says my back wheel may drop off any minute.

"You've got to get that care into the garage before something awful happens. Your engine makes the worst noises I ever heard."

We go for a drive. All I hear is the motor running. She hears worn pistons, tired spark plugs and a dirty carburetor. We're doomed, she informs us, unless we drive to a garage as quickly as possible.

Or better yet, have it towed. You never know when it might fall into a heap of nuts, bolts and headlights right there in the middle of Washington Avenue.

We are doing 70 M.P.H. on I-75. The radio is loud enough so you can't hear the motor running. You can't. But SHE can. "I think you'd better pull into a gas station at the next exit," says the voice of doom as the north bound traffic hurtles northward.

"What's wrong?" I ask, trying not to panic at the wheel. "Am I having a blow-out? Is the motor falling out? Is there still time?"

"You mean you can't hear that chirping noise under the hood?"

"I thought that was background music for the Rolling Stones."

"I told you something was wrong, and you didn't believe me," she recalls when our auto stood crippled in the driveway. "Remember, when I heard that squealing noise under the car, and you said it was just the weather?"

After all, doesn't Van Cliburn know when there is an off sound in his Steinway? And doesn't Leonard Bernstein know right away when there is a rusty flute in his group?

"Get to a gas station right away," she snaps as we pull out of the shopping center.

"You hear something that's going to cost me $50 bucks and the loss of my car for a week?"

"No," she says disgustedly, "the tank is on empty."

The Day Long Breakfast Summer Trademark

Some wise and witty mother (not me, I'm unhappy to say) once called summer the season of the Day-long Breakfast. She spoke well, this unknown parent, because I can say from personal experience that since June 12, or whenever it was that school let out, I have regularly put away the cornflakes as I peeled the supper potatoes.

Yesterday at 3:25 p.m., I had just finished cleaning the kitchen and was about to put away the orange juice when Barbara wandered in. "You didn't feed me yet." She said accusingly. "I did too. I distinctly remember making you a bologna sandwich at 11:30."

"That wasn't my breakfast. That was just a snack while I watched television. You didn't give me any lunch either."

"But you were sitting there at the table with all the other children."

"I don't like pizza for lunch, so I had a peanut butter sandwich and two oranges and a glass of milk. You didn't give me lunch."

"Well what do you call all of that other stuff you ate?"

"That was just to fill me up until I had a really lunch."

"Like what?"

"Like French fries and ketchup." Her big blue eyes filled with tears. So did mine. And then the phone rang.

"It's for me. I'll get it," said Barbara, knocking me to one side and plunging at the telephone. This kid may be starving, but she has a shoulder like Jimmy Brown. It wasn't for her. Mrs. Early from the PTA was on the phone.

"Know what, Mrs. Early," my child wailed into the phone. "It's time for me to watch 'Dark Shadows' already and my mother hasn't given me any breakfast or lunch yet." I snatched the phone from her dimpled little hands and she went out to watch 'Dark Shadows' with the other 20 children who watch it at our house.

Mrs. Early didn't really have much to say. She did mention that the PTA was trying to promote a hot lunch program this fall for children who were not being adequately fed at home. "And I'm sure this will be of great interest to YOU, Mrs. Hansen." I allowed as how it was and wearily hung up. Joe was standing in the kitchen, when I returned. 'Dark Shadows' scares him.

"Hey, Mom, when you fix Barbara's breakfast would you make me some toast to eat while Mr. Magic is on?"

I try not to cuss in front of kids, but I remember screaming a little as I got out the puffed rice and bread.

What's wrong with Barb?

Once in a while the place gets to looking as if Attila the Hun had just broken camp. When this happens, we (the family) sit around looking at it, neatness being a hereditary trait none of the children inherited from their father.

Fearing that someone will complain to the health department, or someone we don't know very well will drop in, we decide mutually that somebody had better clean up the house.

First, though, we must play a family game of long standing called "What's Wrong?" That's when I say to Trisha "Hey, why don't you carry the laundry hampers down to the basement? And she asks, "What's wrong with Barb?"

When she says this, she is not inquiring about her sister's health. As a matter of fact, she knows her sister is in the pink with health.

No, what's wrong with Barb doesn't mean what's WRONG with Barb, it means why can't Barb, and not Trish, carry down the laundry hamper.

For a good 15 minutes or so, the game will revolve around seemingly excellent reasons why neither Barb nor Trish can carry the laundry down to the basement. Meantime, a neighbor drops in to hand over some of our mail which was accidently delivered to her house.

Until moments ago, she was someone we knew only slightly. Now she is our best friend. How come? Because, when I suggested we clean up the house, I distinctly remember also saying, "Good grief, I wouldn't let anybody by my best friend in here right now." Politics makes strange bedfellows. Having the house in a mess begets strange friends.

Anyway, back to the family sitting around the living room getting ready to make plans to clean up the house. Somebody suggests that we form a steering committee who will, in turn, delegate tasks and appoint chairmen.

"To clean up the house?" I hear you ask, clear from here. It's like this, cleaning up our house isn't a task to be taken lightly. We wish it wasn't even a task to be taken at all. But household help costing what it does, we press bravely on.

The steering committee looks over the situation and decides that before any action is taken it will be necessary to appoint a subcommittee to conduct a survey to determine the needs of the house.

The survey committee spends five minutes looking at the unwashed dishes in the sink and returns to the living room with its findings. Yes, the house does need to be cleaned – badly. It would be a good idea to spend about five hours on it.

The family members are indignant. Five hours? There isn't a person in the family with that much time, say the younger ones, with the possible exception of the mother. They caucus and return with a verdict. One hour is all they can afford to spend.

More time is spent selecting a director for housecleaning project – also an assistant director. They agree to work at a salary within the budget, but not much. We come now to the part where we hire the staff. Holly will clean the kitchen.

"What's wrong with Joe?" She responds.

"There's nothing wrong with Joe," she is told. "You were hired because you were best fitted for the job." "OK," she says. "Then I want a salary to go with my special qualifications."

Daughter is a Pack Rat

This is the story of my daughter the pack rat. Some people go through life leaving their outgrown clothing, report cards, "A" papers and first drawings from kindergarten blithely behind them.

Not so my daughter the pack rat. If she ever gets elected first woman president, her memorial library will contain memorabilia going clear back to the first time she ever scribble on a sheet of paper. All lovingly preserved by her faithful old mother.

To everyone else, it looks like a spelling list with two marked wrong. "I'm saving that. Don't throw it away. It's important," she murmurs bending over a water color she is doing on the kitchen table. We'll save that too, of course.

Don't worry. I stuff the paper into the desk drawer which is rapidly difficult to close. From the drawer it will eventually go into a large box and up to the attic. When the attic becomes full we plan to erect a warehouse for her.

Is there a scrap of paper around with some arithmetic figures on it? If it is hers, it will be preserved or we will hear about it. The way we did when we found out all of these rags she had collected were going to be made into a quilt.

She has saved every music book, coloring book, reading readiness test which every passed through her hands. She owned the only Barbie clothes in town which came back in style with the midi last winter.

Added to this are the fat folders of tests and papers she brings home from school each year, her embroidery sets, sewing kits and paint-by-number sets which she insists upon saving after they have been used. "They might come in handy."

She was the only kid I ever knew who baked cookies for the first time and saved six of them for souvenirs of her first bake-off. It took a bit of explaining before she was convinced that there was only a limited amount of time you could save jello.

But we love her and also every scarp and tiny bit of paper, books and doll clothes that come with her, all two tons of the stuff. What worries me is how we are ever going to explain to the many she is to marry about her dowry.

Somewhere in this world is a young boy who is going to grow up and get married, and he is going to marry a girl who will bring into his house every arithmetic paper she has ever completed and brought home from school.

Will he love her enough?

Friends Like You Anyway

I will never forget Holly's definition of a friend written when she was only in the third grade. She said, "A friend is someone who likes you anyway."

Looking back over my life I realized that I have only had five such friends and consider myself lucky. Two moved to distant parts of the country, two died, but I still have one or two and hopefully if I live a long time I will find another someday.

There are so few people in one's life with whom once can trust his most inner thoughts, someone who will "like you anyway." A friend doesn't necessarily agree with everything you say or think or do. It's just that a friend knows and understands.

A friend can and has been a Republican and you can be a radical. She can be an immaculate housekeeper when you are a mess. She can believe in birth control and the two-child family, while you are having a baby every year. It isn't necessarily material things in common which make for this type of deep friendship so much as it is a certain kind of kinship of spirit. A friend likes you anyway.

I think housewives, women who are homebound, need this kind of feminine companionship, probably more than anybody. A thing men do not understand is that it is quite possible to be lonely even if one does have several small children a TV and a telephone for company.

I will always remember my friend who called each morning and we'd proceed to discuss all of the trivia that went into our daily grind. I've even written about it, humorously, I like to think. But it wasn't all that funny. It was my friend's phone calls which kept me from walking up the wall most of the time, when all the children were little.

Husbands, of course, regard this daily phoning as the height of wasted time. Men, evidently, do not need this kind of emotional support, or say they do not anyway. But personally I am all for it and recommend it to every young mother who tells me about her nerves. A conversation with a good friend is worth a bottle of tranquilizers. As the girl who has one.

Another thing a friend does is come over when you are sick and make the coffee and she listens while you tell her what a rat your husband is, only she doesn't agree and she doesn't tell anybody because she knows you really don't think so.

A girl particularly needs this kind of a friend when she is at a time and place in her life when she is convinced that the only thing in the world she does quickly and with excellence is get pregnant. Not every woman is talented this way, but the girl who is will understand what I am talking about.

The other evening I suddenly needed to share my day with someone who'd know right off what kind of day it had been and who'd listen even if it did bore her. She's a friend who likes me anyway. I'm lucky to have her.

Solvent Sibling

We have this one kid we call Money Child. In a family not rich by any standards, surrounded by siblings who never seem to have a dime they can call their own, she remains embarrassingly prosperous.

"Why do you suppose she is richer than we are?" I asked my husband.

"I think it's a talent…like being musical or artistic. Some people have a talent for knowing where the money is," he replied.

He's right. Should the phone ring, Money Child is on top of it in seconds. The others hear sounds of boys in the telephone's chime. Money Child hears the sound of money. She can tell a prospective babysitting job by the way the phone sounds.

We know we will never starve for lack of grocery money. There's always Money Child and her cache of riches, wherever she hides it. We can borrow (at 20% interest) whenever we are in need.

I have developed a theory that there really is such a thing as the Midas touch. And it is like sex appeal, you must be born with it. Money Children are born that way. Most of us are doomed to spend our lives toiling to keep body and soul together. Others, like Money Child, could plant a tree and have it spring up blossoming $20 dollar bills.

50

Another thing I have noticed about Money Children is that they are very careful with their money. They never spend it on nonessentials like lunches or school yearbooks. They are good about delegating such responsibility to the proper persons…their parents.

But let anyone in the family so much as breathe the words "shopping center," and there is Money Child, wads of money in her jeans, ready to go out and buy more jeans.

I was never a money child. It was my brother who was rich in our family. While the rest of us spent our time grass-hoppering, he busied himself being an ant and piling up the shekels, which he'd lend the rest of us at bloodletting interest.

He had a bank account before I even found out what a bank was for, and he was two years younger.

"Why don't you go out and earn money like your brother?" my folks would ask me.

"But that would mean that I'd have to work, and I'm sure there must be an easier way."

What I had in mind of course, was this terribly rich man who was someday going to be so bowled over by my beauty that he'd marry me and keep me in diamonds and money for the rest of my ageless life, and I'd never have to work again.

As you know, it didn't turn out that way. Although, I haven't exactly had to toil myself into a basket case, I never got terribly rich. When we are short of cash we can always turn to Money Child, who isn't bothering to wait around for some rich man to marry her and keep her in diamonds. But with her luck she'll probably find him.

Only two will ever hear this music again

I was never one to shed tears when a child went off to kindergarten – I rather like beginnings. Instead, I reserve my tender feelings for the day a youngster graduates from high school and closes another chapter in our family chronicles.

And there is this little pang of sadness – a fleeting passage of down-time before we reopen the book of life and begin a new chapter.

I know I'll feel this pain in a couple of weeks when Holly turns in the regal black and white uniform she's worn so proudly as commander of the Bridgeport High School band. Before the month has ended, she'll turn from one of the most devoted band kids who ever yelled out a lusty, "Band-ten-hut!" into a college-bound young woman.

With childish things she'll pack away her lists of fellow students who carried flags and rifles in the band shows. Into a box for the attic she will place souvenirs from places she's traveled, letters from friends she made along the way and patches bearing the insignias of bands from other schools.

Next year the skirt that swirled gracefully with her every move will swirl with equal grace around the knees of a new commander. She's keeping the tall black English riding boots that have paraded up streets from Florida to Wisconsin.

Other things I expect she will keep with her are those intangible qualities which once assumed, can never be abandoned.

She'll keep the lovely way she walks, the proud tilt of her head and the perky manner she has of twirling about on one foot. She will keep the friends she has made, memories of cross country bus tips, bedding down on strange gymnasium floors and sack lunches eaten at expressway rest stops.

And she will hang onto what she has learned of self-discipline, the strong spirit of community and sense of how personal experience contributes to the common good. All of these things will go with her to college and remain usable commodities for as long as she lives.

A few mementos I plan to keep myself. Like memories of the days when our lives revolved around the band schedule taped to the kitchen wall; days when I shared the feelings of another loyal band parent who remarked, "I have this feeling that if the Lord should call me away today, I'd have to say, 'wait until I check the band schedule first to see if I can work it in.'"

I'll carry forever the feel of her warm tears on my neck as I comforted her when the band "lost," (her definition of placing second in a competition). And I won't forget her victorious homecomings when she stumbled jubilantly into the house, toting her bedroll and boot bags, hoarse from shouting commands.

There were party trips to faraway places with parents of other band kids, cheering in grandstands, pizzas and hamburgers at two in the morning, hiking three-mile parade routes and thinking, "I'm too old to be doing this."

It's the end of a chapter, the beginning of another, a small pause to turn another page.

But for the rest of my life I know that whenever I say the magic words "competition band," I'll raise a picture of a beautiful child in military black and white marching forever to music only she and I will ever hear again.

Times change for princesses

They spent their early years in an 11-room house, where each could have had her own private space had she wished. But from the beginning the three little girls chose to share the biggest bedroom in the house.

At the time it was because they regarded the old house as "spooky," especially upstairs at night. They reasoned that spooks rarely hang around crowds, so not only did they share the room; they augmented their numbers with lots of guests.

With this conditioning to dorm-style living, they had no trouble at all adjusting to the 20-foot master bedroom when the family moved to a new house. The spacious room with its three big windows, black shag carpet and two closets was just the place for three sleeping princesses.

We filled it with the old bedroom furniture enameled sunny lemon yellow and put a yellow rug shaped like a big footprint in the center of the room. On the wall a yellow felt banner said in big black letters, "Promises, Promises, Promises."

Though they shared sleeping quarters, you could never have accused them of being like peas in a pod. They had separate friends, different talents, and didn't even wear the same size clothes. But in succession each initiated the next into the rites of passage of young womanhood.

I used to stop by the bedroom door on Sunday mornings to look at the three sleeping princesses in their yellow rattan beds. The oldest slept on her tummy, like a crumpled doll, just as she had in babyhood.

The second was so completely covered with the blanket, it took a second look to make sure she was there, and the youngest clutched a small security pillow.

The room was always filled with piles of jeans and t-shirts. Posters on the walls proclaimed gentle thoughts of love and life. Jewelry hanging on the mirrors, stuffed animals in the corners and old Seventeen magazines said that this was the domain of young females.

In olden day fairy tales, it was the prince who left to seek lady love or a fortune or to do brave deeds. But times have changed. So in time each liberated princess left the security of the yellow bedroom for a life of her own.

One went away to marry her childhood sweetheart. The second left home to establish a place of her own. And, as in fairy tales of yore, the youngest and most adventurous journeyed thousands of miles from home for a new kind of life. No longer do princesses sit around in castles waiting for the prince on a white horse to show up.

All that remains are some tattered posters, a few discarded pieces of clothing and a haunting, sweet fragrance that lingers in the room as I move my own belongings in there. I carefully folded the bright yellow banner and put it on one of those shelves you reserved for things you no longer need but cannot bear to discard.

Why did I ever think young princesses stay young forever?

Promises, promises, promises.

Cub Scouts have grown smarter

It's our Joe's turn to be a Cub Scout, and our final (we hope) experience with the Blue and Gold comes when we are also grandparents and thankfully past the age when neither of us feels we must leap to our feet volunteering every time the Cub Master opens his mouth. This we leave to the young, strong parents whose oldest child is 8 and not 28.

Can a middle-aged woman survive menopause and den meetings at the same time? The answer is no, so I just don't try. Also Joe's father and I have discovered that as we've grown older somehow Cub Scouts have grown smarter.

Last spring Joe came home from his den meeting with a block of wood 2 ½ inches square and 7 inches long. He also had some sandpaper, 4 wheels, 1 axle and a sheet of simple detailed easy-to-follow instructions. "I have to build a racing car for Cub Scouts," he announced.

"Great," said I. "There's an empty table in the back room you can work at."

"But Dad has to help me. My den mother said Cub Scouts are for boys and their parents."

"Yeah. I'd forgotten about that part. But as long as it's your dad who had to help get a racing care out of that wood and not me it's all right."

"Make a template the size of your projected vehicle," said the instructions.

"What's a template?" I asked my husband.

"I know what it is, and that's all that is important right now. Joe, come out in the kitchen and watch Daddy make a template for Cub Scouts," yelled Daddy.

"I can't. I'm watching the Lucy Show," he called form the TV room. "What's a template? I thought you were making me a racing car."

"This is supposed to be a father-son project. Now get out here and start sanding."

"After Lucy."

"What's it mean to sand groove down the center?" I asked my husband as I read the simple, detailed, easy-to-follow instructions for building a Cub Scout model racing car.

"You'll see when I get to it. It's kind of difficult to explain."

"Oh, but it is something any 8-year-old boy could understand I gather," I said.

"Keep your smart remarks to yourself," he snarled.

"How come we've only got one axle for this darn thing," Himself wanted to know after he'd worked on his father-son racing car for about a week.

"I had two but one fell out of my pocket, "Joe replied. "I thought you could make me another one." He went out to ride his bike.

A week later we attended a Pack meeting. Joe's father's racing car didn't win a prize.

"The other kids' dads made better racing cars then you did," said Joe.

"Well maybe next time the project will be knocked down Rolls Royce complete with easy-to-follow blueprints. Just the thing for a 9-year-old boy. Then I'll really shoe them," said Joe's father.

Mud and Memories

I didn't see the creature when he came to our door, but I found the shell of it had dropped in a sodden heap on the garage floor, where its father made it strip before it came in to get a bath.

We thought we had seen the last of the bad weather which flooded the basements, backyards and family rooms. But no. Last Friday, a day off for school boys, a good deal of it came to visit getting no further than the door.

The Abominable Mud Person had once been a reasonably clean, recognizable youngster. It was hard to believe they were one and the same, if I am to believe the father of the once reasonably clean and recognizable child, who was home when the Abominable Mud Person rang the doorbell.

It took three cycles of the washer to remove the mud from the snorkel jacket, socks and jeans. It took two washes in the bathtub to clean the mud from the half-filled snowmobile boots. All of the said items were carefully transferred into the house in a pail.

Underneath the shell of mud was a happy small boy who had spent a wonderful day of hiking in the woods, looking for the herd of small deer that roam our territory. He'd been raised in the city where the closest thing to high adventure was getting to the store and back without having his money stolen from him.

Adventure out here can be had in the woods and open fields, where there are lightning bugs to catch at twilight on warm summer nights. Adventure is looking out the window at dawn on a fall day to find a thousand birds traveling south had landed in the fields behind the house.

Exploits come in the form of riding a horse for the first time, fishing in the Cass River, sleeping out all night in the woods without being afraid and feeding wild ducks in a nearby pond.

Other delights include being able to skate in the backyard and occasionally meeting pheasants and rabbits who do not mind sharing open meadows with boys and dogs. Some youngsters have known about meadows and wild der and riding horseback through woods since they were tiny. This boy has only known about them for a little more than half a year.

And this is why, although we joked a little about the Abominable Mud Person who appeared at our door last Friday, nobody said much to the boy underneath. The years of growing up and going away are already at hand and there is still so much to be discovered in so short a time.

Little One during his finest hour

The golden oldie spiritual, "All God's Chillun Got Shoes" has always had a personal meaning for me. In the days when the Old South ran exclusively on slave power, chillum having shoes was indeed a miracle. It was one around our house, too, for a long time.

The miracle was that I continued taking my children to the shoe store year in and year out – a chore I found almost as unappealing as cleaning the stove. The difference is you can keep lighting a stove until it catches fire. If you fail to buy shoes and you can afford it, you're in big trouble.

Buying shoes for Little One was especially painful in light of his need to choose the most outlandish, least durable shoes in the place and his talent for doing it.

"Let your child start making decisions early," was the warning in my child-care book. Let him! He came into the world making decisions at the top of his lungs, and he particularly like to make them in shoe stores. Most of his choices were bad, but as a show of decision-making in general, it was Little One's finest hour.

Before we left for the store, Little One and I had our usual pre-shoe-buying talk. Naturally he agreed with everything I said so I wouldn't draw a picture of his foot and take it down and pick his shoes out myself.

Little One's shoes, I pointed out to him, had to be waterproof to withstand walking daily in ditches shin-deep in water. They had to be impervious to mud; snow, wet cement and whatever had been left in his path by stray dogs. Little One's attitude was walk through life, not around it. His shoes were his testimony.

It wasn't enough hat his shoes be sturdy. They also had to be easily cleaned up for Sundays and quick drying between daily wearings. He had another pair of canvas shoes for what his teacher called "physical education" and he called "gym days." They were to be kept in pristine condition, but nothing about Little One was ever pristine.

For one thing, he often had to wear the canvas shoes between gym days when his other ones were in dry dock. And he never, never wore his boots. It wasn't manly, he said. He liked cowboy boots which shed a heel after a month, high laced boots which took most of the morning to lace and shoes guaranteed to self-destruct after two wearings.

I've always looked back on Little One's shoes as a test of how much stress I can put up without retreating into a gibbering madness. The answer, I found, is quite a bit.

I can't help wondering though, how the United States Army is coping with his field boots.

Little One's nature wasn't geared to camp

"You just don't know how far you've come from the basics until your child goes away to camp for the first time." Speaking was a young mother sitting at a picnic table, a bottle of ketchup and some potato salad away from where I sat eavesdropping on her tale of her son's first camp encounter and remembering our little one's first reply to the call of the wild.

Actually, it wasn't his reply, it was his parents'. We decided that by age 10, it was high time our sheltered youngest son learned about nature and all that healthy stuff. I had to agree with the young mother on the other side of the ketchup bottle. We are certainly shaped by our surroundings.

Little One was a true product of his environment and had been raised a far cry from the basics his older brothers once reveled in. His only swimming holes were the heated pools back at the "Y" and those in friends' back yards. His idea of roughing it was to move the television set closer to the open patio door or getting more than four miles from a drive-in hamburger stand.

By the time he set off for Camp Kemo Sabi, his only brush with the north country was the time he went with us to spend a week at the Park Place Hotel in Traverse City and he discovered one basic -- room service.

No camper in the world ever went off to discover the joys of camping more poorly prepared than our little one. So his first letter from camp, while disappointing, didn't surprise us much.

"Dear Mom and Dad, they make us go in this crummy freezing lake every day. It's freezing to death and there's a lot of guckky stuff in the bottom. I'll probably die."

Two days later we received another note from the doomed one of Camp Kemo Sabi and things were looking even worse. There being no room service, hunger was beginning to set in.

"Dear Mom and Dad, I'm starving to death. All the food is crummy and they don't let us buy snacks until night so I have to wait until after supper to get anything good to eat."

Not only were they trying to freeze and poison him in an unheated lake with no chlorine in it to kill germs, they were denying him "good food" like candy bars, his staple at that age.

But things were getting worse. He informed us in his final letter, that is, the last one he wrote home before we picked him up, not his dying message -- although it sounded like one.

"Dear Mom and Dad, I'll be glad when you pick me up. They're always making us go on long, long hikes and look at bugs. Then they make us go in the crummy, freezing lake. I hope I don't get all worn out. Can we stop at McDonald's on the way home?"

We drove north to gather up the prisoner and his duffle bag. Fully expecting to have to rush a living skeleton to the nearest hamburger and fries headquarters. For someone who'd been starved, frozen, gone on forced marches and been terrified by bugs, he looked surprisingly fit and had even made friends with a couple of other over-civilized youngsters.

I'd like to close this by saying Little One's camping experience made a new child out of him and that henceforth he was a true child of the woods. But I can't and still be truthful.

Fortified by a double order of fries, he arrived home strong enough to call his best buddy and suggest a swim in their heated, guck-free pool.

He never went to camp again. But that doesn't mean he was off the north country for life. Before the week was out, he was ready for the new summer adventure.

"Hey, Mom," he said one evening after supper, "Why don't we all go up to that hotel next week. I could watch TV on the balcony and call room service whenever I'm hungry. It'd be really neat."

Little One has gone

"Where's Little One?"

His father and I were sitting in our living room on one of those quiet Sunday afternoons we seem to be enjoying more and more often these days.

Little One might have been at the neighbor's house watching television. He could have been upstairs in his room, talking on the phone or out riding his 10-speed bike around the subdivision. A child's horizons have a way of widening imperceptibly until they suddenly disappear from a parent's view.

And it was while thinking about this I suddenly realized that Little One, he of the incredible childhood adventures, funny sayings and ragtag jeans, wasn't around anymore. In a passage of time which now seems no longer than a sigh, he had left us.

Upstairs, in his red, white and blue bedroom, The Teen-ager's rock albums, paperback books and empty Coke cans are piled atop Little One's abandoned books about railroads and dinosaurs.

In the basement Little One's electric train and its toy village lie forgotten on their table, unnoticed except when some grown-up friends try to return to their own childhood for a little while. Nearby some Matchbox cars, plastic cowboys and horses wait forlornly to be played with.

Sometimes a visiting child will get them out and we think what a waste. "Why don't we give Little One's old toys away to someone who'd enjoy them?" we ask the Teen-ager once in a while.

"I want to keep them in case I ever have a little kid of my own," he replies selfishly.

Upstairs, in his closet are hangers filled with Little One's outgrown clothes and on the floor beneath them a stack of outgrown games and old school papers. Maybe we should do something with those too, I tell his father as we sit in our living room on quiet Sunday afternoons.

I suppose we have known for quite a while that Little One wasn't going to stay around forever. Awareness dawned gradually as he insisted we abandon childish things like stockings hung at Christmas and money from the Tooth Fairy.

And when was the last time we bothered to hire a babysitter or fix an Easter basket or bring home a toy from the supermarket? At what exact moment in our lives did Little One go away and the Teen-ager come to stay?

Oh, not that the Teen-ager isn't welcome in our home. He's a good looking, poised young man who plays in the school band and likes girls and tacks posters on his bedroom wall. We are happy with him and the promise he gives us of the adult he will soon become.

It's just that until the day when his father asked where Little One had gone, I hadn't realized that without our even noticing, he'd slipped into our memory world to be with other children who have grown up and left their toys for us to put away.

Herb, Ralph, Jeanette, Steve, John

Trish, Barb, Holly, Joe

Chapter 3: Marriage

REALLY, this advice is for your own good - back when I was a bride...

Back when I was a bride and struggling to master the art of housewifery (much of which has eluded me to this day); I was frequently visited by one unwelcomed female relative.

What made her so unwelcomed was that if she happened to find me sweeping the floor she would snatch my broom from my hands saying briskly, "Here, let me show you how to REALLY use a broom." When she had raised a cloud of dust deep enough to shroud an aircraft carrier, she would kindly return the broom and inform me in tones of smug righteousness - "There now. That's the way you sweep a floor."

I was very young then and too timid to suggest she borrow the broom for a ride home. So when the dust settled, and she discovered that it had not yet choked me to death, I was usually treated to an impressive recital of how hard she had to work and how tired she got. I'll bet she did!

But you learn something from everyone and I even learned something from her which was how not to sweep a floor and how not to treat young brides when I got to be an experienced older woman.

Next to the broom-snatching types, if there is anyone else thoroughly detested by struggling young wives it is relatives who give advice. Relatives with unasked for advice seem prone to descend upon young couples with ideas about everything from their budgets to their sex lives. And they are not loved for it.

Unsolicited opinions are always preceded by such statements as, "I'm not one to give unasked for advice," or "I hope you won't be offended if I say this," or "I wouldn't say anything, but it's for your own good."

And there is the older relative with nothing to do. Her home is in apple pie order, with no one around but her husband who only dares muss up an occasional ash tray. With time on her hands, she visits a young mother of three preschoolers who all have measles. If the young mother is also pregnant, has been up all night with the kids and needs some help with the dishes her older relative is so helpful. But here is what she offers by way of encouragement. "Oh you young mothers are all alike today. You don't have it so hard with all the modern conveniences they have now. In my day, we really had to work."

But she is nice enough to leave quickly because she doesn't want to be a bother. And of course she would never dream of offering to stay awhile and help out. Not that she doesn't have plenty of time, but she is just not the type who interferes.

Truthfully, what kind of older relative are you to the young couples in your family? Now you know I'm not one to give unasked for advice, and I hope you won't be offended because I said this. Really, I wouldn't have said anything at all about it. But it's for your own good.

Side note from Betty: *"I don't think today's young woman would put up with this stuff. But, it was my generation in the 1960s who broke down those conventions."*

Sewer, storm foil crime and evidence is returned

In the words of comedian Sid Caesar, "War is heck." And I think this is one reason why so many women will go to such lengths to avoid a fight with their husbands, particularly over money matters.

Take this experience of a dear friend, whose good name I will protect with my life, and who is married to the type of man who just can't understand why she might need $100 winter suit marked down to $60 in the middle of May. Nor can he understand why she would need it badly enough to charge it when they both agreed to cut out the charge accounts for a while. But charge it she did, and then hid the purchase in the back of the closet until she could safely break the news to the lord of the house.

The bill arrived on a steamy June afternoon when the only really appropriate suit would have been a bikini. My friend tore off the heading of the bill which she needed to pay her account. Then she stashed it in her handbag, then, wondering what to do with the rest of the evidence, she promptly folded and flushed it away.

That evening our heroine enjoyed a tepid shower, a cold drink and went to bed with a light heart, secure in the knowledge that she had committed the perfect crime. She was so relaxed she didn't even bother staying up for the 11:00 p.m. TV weather report. Sometime later, around 1:30 a.m. the worst summer storm in 20 years descended on the town. During the storm the TV antenna was hit by lightning and the basement flooded knee deep.

Of course this was her husband's problem. The wife with the hidden suit had all she could do that morning trying to remember how to make coffee with the old fashioned percolator on the gas stove. There was no electricity. Even toast would be a problem. So she was only dimly aware of her man as he passed the kitchen, in pajamas and wading boots on his way to the basement for a look.

He descended, returned almost immediately, wearing a look Moses may have had when he climbed down from Mt. Sinai, the first time.

"This should prove once and for all whose side the Lord is on around this house," hubby said. And he handed her the bill for her suit which had somehow backed up through the sewer pipe and was floating around in the basement overflow.

I think that this story has a moral: Never, ever dispose of a bill in such a sneaky, underhanded fashion unless you are sure of both the plumbing and the forces of nature. Remember it's not for nothing that severe storms are referred to as "acts of God."

The time of the sauerkraut

One time we made sauerkraut. Someone died and left us a five gallon crock, a cabbage cutter and a 25 pound rock. It's the only thing we've ever inherited so naturally we were delighted.

The time was September, the weather chilly and visions of apples in the cellar danced through our wee little heads. And then we saw an ad for cabbage by the bushel. "My dad used to make sauerkraut," recalled Himself. "He kept it out in the garage. It was delicious."

Well nothing brings back the good old days like a hankering for the sauerkraut you Dad used to make, so we bought a bushel of cabbage and 10 pounds of coarse salt. Next morning I called a friend of German extraction and got a tried and true recipe of sauerkraut.

It would have gone off rather well I think if it had not been for "this guy at work." There is a surplus of experts where my husband works, and 50% of the confusion around here stems from their advice. This particular expert claimed you didn't need a recipe for sauerkraut. "He says you just dump in two handfuls of salt for every handful of cabbage. He makes it every year. It always turns out.

Naturally if this guy's sauerkraut was an every year success ours would be too. We shredded the cabbage and tossed it into the crock with handfuls and handfuls of salt. When the crock was filled we put an old plate on top and weighed it down with the rock. We were in the basement at the time. "OK," I said, "Now carry it out to the garage like your dad used to do." "Oh you always are the wittiest girl," said Himself. "That's why I married you."

"Well we can't let it sit here in the middle of the basement all winter." "That is true. It has to age for about a month. We'd better slide it into a corner someplace." You have no idea how heavy a crock of sauerkraut is. But together we shoved it into the unused coal room at the rear of our Michigan basement.

After a month we went down to see the sauerkraut. We didn't need a light to locate it. By the dim glow of the 25 watt bulb it looked awful. "You taste it." "I'm afraid." He tasted and gagged. "I think it needs to set a while longer." Another month passed. This time we just peeked under the plate. The sauerkraut was taking longer than we had thought, and Mother took to dropping off cans of air freshener whenever she came over.

Eventually we forgot about the sauerkraut if you can believe it. Once a year we'd look in the coal room but neither of us knew what to do with it. It was like having an insane aunt locked up in the attic. We didn't dare turn it loose or try to keep it.

Then one day a man who was down there fixing the wiring kicked the crock over and it broke. He was terribly apologetic about it. "There wasn't anything in it but an old plate and a rock and some straw." He said. "Oh it's alright; it was just an old thing that's been down there for years." I said. "Really we'll never miss it."

It had in fact been seven years. But we still have the cabbage cutter around in case we ever decide to have another go at sauerkraut making.

Actions speak louder than words

Body language isn't so new. That unspoken jargon that is supposed to let others know what we are thinking without having to come right out and say it, has been around for years.

My husband Herb, isn't given to a lot of useless, idle talk has been using body language for years. Like when we go to a party and he wants to go home early and he will let me know when that is. The other guests won't know because he isn't about to walk over to me and snarl, "C'mon, let's get out of here."

"I'll look across the room and raise my eyebrows….like this...and you'll know that I am ready to leave the party," he says before the party.

"OK, and when I look like I'm not seeing you raise your eyebrows because I'm admiring the hostess' new card table, you will know that I'm NOT ready to leave the party."

"I'll go along with that. I'm not unreasonable, even if I'm not crazy about cocktail parties. If I see you meditating on the coffee table I'll wait another 30 minutes and then I'll say, "Remember, we've got to get up early tomorrow.""

"And then when you hear me telling the woman next to me that we plan to sleep in tomorrow you will get the message that I still don't want to leave."

Or could it be the other way around. His hanging around the good looking divorcee in the silver jumpsuit tells me that I think it would be a good time to leave the party.

My hanging around by the front door wearing my coat, holding his coat and galoshes, is supposed to tell him this too. On the other hand when he gets up and wanders out to the kitchen, is a clear indication that he has decided he is having a better time at the party than he expected to have, so let's stay and enjoy ourselves.

Driving to our last party he came up with a new version of the body language that tells us when to leave the party. "Honey, when you look across the room and see me sleeping on the sofa with an empty glass in my hand can I count on you to get the message?"

"Which is…?"

"That I've passed out waiting for you to decide you've been at the party long enough and you'll have to drive home."

Little Discussions

In the history of nearly every family on the block you are likely to find a share of old family figures of speech which remain forever to be called forth when things remind us of how they got started.

I'm thinking in particular of the time Patricia was in 5th grade and her teacher was inspired to have each of the students write an essay on their family lives. She helpfully furnished them with a list of questions covering everything from how the parents treated each other to what they had for dinner.

Personally I think this was a sneaky Pete way of finding out about things that were none of her business…but no matter, on with my story.

We came off rather well in our biography according to Patricia, who merely said of her family, "My mother and father never fight, the just have little discussions and we have a usual diet."

Behind this laconic statement was the truth: Whenever Himself and I are engaged in a round of hot dispute and one of the kids says "stop fighting," we always tell them, "Mommy and Daddy aren't fighting. We're having a little discussion."

Amid broken crockery and negotiations for custody of the cats, a family figure of speech was born. Now whenever we view a full-scale riot on the 6 o'clock news or a war in the Middle East someone will remark, "They're not fighting. They're just having a little discussion."

Today, if we learn of someone existing on a diet of brown rice and tea or spending a week in the woods living on grubs and lily bulbs she is said to be eating "a usual diet."

We found ourselves with another figure of speech during those times when one child would torment another and turning to us, his parents, say over his victim's screams, "but all I was doing was patting him on the head."

The tormentor knew full well that if there was anything in the world the tormented one couldn't stand it was a pat on the head. So whenever we see anyone being hit where it hurts that person most deeply, we like to say, "Well, as Paris said when the carried away Achilles, "But all I did was shoot him in the heel."

And I can't leave this column without telling you about the family monster who keeps us from doing anything we don't want to do.

He was born several years ago when a prefers-to-be-anonymous son was 5 years old and afraid to go upstairs alone. "I can't," he'd announce at bedtime. "A monster might get me."

"How about running up to the hardware store for me, honey," himself asked as I settled down with a Saturday afternoon book, "I can't," I replied, "a monster might get me."

All of a sudden it was time for us to have another one of our little discussions. It was one of our better ones, I must say.

Season's End

There's bittersweet growing near the place where he's buried and a maple tree that will quietly turn to sunlit gold and scarlet before it dies for the winter. And, in a sense, they tell our story.

To lose a partner, a lover, a husband after 35 years is akin to finding half of yourself cut away and discarded. And for a while after he died, I'd find myself going from place to place thinking I'd find this half any minute.

During the last weeks of his illness, I told myself, this isn't happening, and like others before I prayed and begged and bargained with God to give him one more chance at life.

A young person I know, recently divorced, said to me, "Of all the things I never pictured in my future life, I never thought of myself as divorced."

And I said, "I know. I never thought of myself as a widow, either. I'd always thought I'd die first and he'd be left with the pain." But life does not always offer us options, if indeed it ever does. Our only choice is between courage and cowardice, between grace and chaos.

Our last summer together spent itself in a luxury of scenes which, even now, come to me unbidden, like flower fragrances drifting through an open window at night.

A small river in the town of Dundee, with glimpses of baby ducks nestling on the banks…Walking hand in hand through the town and saying…"In our next life let's live in a town with hills around it."…Crossing the blue bridge in Cincinnati which separates Kentucky from Ohio and immediately getting lost. "If there's a bridge to be crossed anyplace, Betty will cross it, no matter what." He told our companions.

Memories of skies, lakes and trees in Northern Michigan return as blurred impressions of blue and green washed in gold. And looking back, I remember again and again the tiny psychic voice inside that whispered, "Hang on to this, and keep it forever."

The last day we spent up north we accepted a boat ride from a young couple we knew slightly, pleasant people who were to share with us the last good times. Fifteen miles out on Grand Traverse Bay we found an island, wooded and quiet as the first morning of Eden.

Walking through the woods, whispering so as not to frighten the deer and their fawns feeding nearby, we talked about the goodness of being a couple once more, the way we'd been before the children filled our lives to the bring. I said, "Why don't we try to come back here again next year." And he only said, "We'll see, next year."

Later that evening we walked around Traverse City in the rain, eating cherries from paper cups, recalling the good days and the bad. In the end it was a true marriage of mind and spirit, a remembrance of what it was that had caught and held us together through all the years. But it was the end.

For many days I refused to cry in front of my children believing they needed me to be strong. But a priest said to me, "Tears are a gift from God, do not be afraid to share them." And after that our family wept together.

Returning from Traverse City on the last day of our summer, I remember asking him to drive very slowly by the bay; my last glimpse until next year. I tried to see the island but it was too far away, and already too many things were getting in our way.

I should have known.

After grief, inevitable rebirth November

"For everything there is a season, and a time for every matter under heaven: a time to be born, and a time to die...a time to break down, and a time to build up...a time to weep, and a time to laugh...a time to mourn, and a time to dance..." Ecclesiastes 3

This morning, for the first time in many weeks, I watched the coming of daylight and was happy to see the sun rise. And at the same time I knew that somewhere deep inside me the spirit we call "self" had begun to heal.

Why did I ever doubt that it would? Why did I wonder if a time would come again when I'd awake in happy, hopeful anticipation of the day ahead? For a long time now I've been thinking that expectations of contentment die along with love.

Have you ever wondered how the spirit knows when it is time for healing? Who tells it? From whom or where comes this silent message:

"The time for deep sorrow is almost past. You should have known this from the beginning and trusted. It's true, there will be other times when the bottom falls out of your life, when you wish you could roll back the days and replay the life script the way it should have been written.

"But these moments will be fewer as time passes. Life is still good, and there is yet much of it to be lived."

Once, after my husband died, I asked someone if I could ever drive to work full of expectation of good things ahead...the pleasure of my job...the sights of the waking world as I passed by.

Seeing children waiting for school buses, the changing of the seasons played out day by day in the woods on the edge of town, and wondering where everyone was going, to what jobs and experiences, as we set out so early each morning.

So many of the things the two of us loved are not things from which I can run away...going outside to watch sunsets, enjoying the beauty of cool summer mornings and the snow-muffled sanctuary of deep winter nights.

You can hid from friends and relatives, run away from human experience and put behind you the day-to-day habits you once thought would continue forever. But there is no turning away from the small garden outside the back door as it dies in the October chill.

It is possible, I've discovered, slowly and painfully, to lose the green days of summer in the cold gray mornings of late fall. And possible also for sorrow to quietly slip away with the passing of time.

How do we know when the transition starts? At what moment in winter do we step outside and a softness in the air tells us that there will be more bleak days ahead, but they are becoming fewer?

So often I have wondered who or what tells a baby it is time to be born. Who carries a message to the crocuses that it is finally safe to peek above the ground?

I remember once when I was seriously ill following childbirth, knowing I'd passed the crisis and everything was going to be all right. No doctor or nurse came into my hospital room to tell me this. It wasn't even daylight. I simply awoke, still very ill, but knowing I'd get better soon.

Who can say from where comes the message that it is time for the beginning or the end of life, or when it is time for rebirth? I've only come to believe firmly it is a voice to which we should listen and one to be trusted.

Ghosts of summer past haunt north country

Sometimes I think I'd like to visit Traverse City at Cherry Festival time just once more - buying cherries from vendors on the streets, waiting with our friends for the sound of marching bands coming up the street. Laughing, telling jokes, getting sunburned and drinking lukewarm soda pop.

I might spend another night partying in rooms at the Park Place Hotel, meeting for breakfast in the dining room, sitting on balconies with swim suits drying over the railings, calling down to newcomers in the parking lot.

Sometimes I think I'll go back to Houghton Lake again, driving a station wagon loaded with children and cats and food and clothing for a week's stay at Windermere Lodge. In the cool of the morning I'll stand on the porch and watch the baby robins in the eaves getting up the nerve to fly away.

Afternoons we can sit on the shore, visiting with companionable people from other cottages, reading and drinking gin and tonics, the smell of Coppertone suntan lotion hanging over the scene.

We'll make our usual plans to come back next year together so things will be just the same as they are now. We'll try not to notice how the children playing in the water are growing up as we grow older.

At dusk I'll walk back to the shore alone to watch the lights across the lake blink on one by one and follow the red-light path of a fishing boat moving across the darkening water to a home port someplace off to the east of me.

Maybe on one of my days up north I'll drive to Petoskey and maybe, this time the emerald hills and turquoise lakes glimpsed through fringes of pine trees won't fade before I've imprinted them on my memory forever. I'll turn off the air conditioner and roll down the car windows and let the wind blow in, filling it with the sweet evergreen smell of the North Country.

Along the way I'll pass the cottage signs - signs which let me know that humans are not too far away. "We're Here." "The Hughes's," "Sunny Point," and the ever popular "Dew Drop Inn." Cottage signs are notable for everything, but originality.

I never did know any of the owners of these places. But their signs at the edge of the road were like pebbles on a trail, small signals that the highway I'm traveling is a familiar one. I am not lost.

On one hot, sunny afternoon, I'll stand for a while on the shore of Lake Michigan, watching a streamer moving slowly along the horizon until it disappears and wonder, as always, where it's going.

I'll smell the fishy smell that tells me, even in the dark, that I'm near a lake. At night I'll walk back to my cottage through dark, warm sand listening to conversations coming through cabin windows. Later I'll lie in bed in a room that's treetop high and go to sleep hearing wind rushing through evergreens and waves lapping on sand.

I would celebrate the North Country if I went there, revel in its lush greenness, meditate on the edge of the water and watch the children in red plastic lifesavers scampering on the beach. I'd party once again at the Park Place Hotel and wait on the sunlit streets of Traverse City for the parade to pass.

I would do all of these things if it were not for the memories of other times that I know would come rushing in to crowd the present into a mere shadow. The bands and floats in the Cherry Festival Parade would dim before the bright ghosts of parades and music past, and my parties haunted by spirits of the past revelry with other friends.

Visions of those other small children who played on the beach and ran to my side would come, as they often do anyway, and, with their joyful, luminous presence, block my view of children who now make sand castles and splash at the water's edge with their plastic toys.

I could sit on the beach once more with companionable people drinking gin and tonic, reading and talking. But I know I'd run out of things to say and fall to wondering about those other ones who have gone their own way as I have gone mine.

And at night I'd lie awake alone, in a bedroom that's tree top high and listen to the winds of the past rushing through the evergreens outside the open window, drowning out the sounds of tonight.

I thought maybe I'd go back up north this summer - just once more. But I know I won't. Up north is haunted.

Betty and Herb

Chapter 4: Parenting

'It's Probably Just a Bug That's Been Going Around'

Do you panic at the first symptoms of the flu, or are you the type who stays bravely on the job until the ambulance arrives? I am a coward who collapses into bed with the first sniffle, but my husband is a noble soul who refuses to recognize illness the way the U.N. ignores Red China. His stock diagnosis for anything from a headache to extreme rigor mortis is that the patient is either imagining things or is, for some mysterious reason deliberately malingering. But somehow, between us, we manage to maintain an odd sort of balance when one of us is, or THINKS he is ill.

While I am getting ready for a mad dash to the hospital emergency room my hero walks around comfortingly suggesting that we try and see if the patient can't "fight it off." "You worry too much," he says. "It's probably this little bug that's been going around. I've had the same thing myself all week." The idea is, of course, that I should put on a stiff upper lip and keep going too, even if I might be dying. In fact the only illness, if they can be called that, which he ever recognized as not completely imaginary were my nine pregnancies.

At one point in my long and busy life I existed in an almost continuous state of expectation. I had a wardrobe of maternity clothes for every season, and our kindly family physician looked upon me not as a patient but as a guaranteed annuity. I was used to having people ask, "Is this again or yet?"

There was one particular time when I was feeling especially rotten for no reason that I knew of. It was nothing I could put my finger on, just a general feeling of "all-overishness." I considered trying to "fight it off." But my cowardly impulses surfaced once more so I went to the doctor, convinced that I would be told I was wasting away from some newly discovered disease. The doctor checked me carefully and to my complete astonishment congratulated me and wrote my due date on his calendar.

That evening when my husband came home from work, I was lying on the sofa, looking wan and ill, which indeed I was, and reading the new spring catalogue. He felt my forehead to see if I was feverish and was his usual tender and sympathetic self. "Oh, you're all right," he said briskly. "What you've got is this thing everybody's been catching lately. I've had the same thing all week myself."

I smiled cryptically and turned the pages of the catalogue to the section on maternity clothes. "If that's true, you will never have to work again, dear," I murmured.

Live dangerously – be a parent

Accident rates for various occupations are intriguing, particularly if the occupation is your own. You know, without being told, a dynamite handler's job is riskier than that of a secretary in most cases. But statistics gatherers are surprisingly silent about the accident rates for parents. This bothers me.

Trust me, I speak of what I know when I tell you raising a family is a high-risk job, comparable to defusing bombs and painting water towers.

I still recall (with a twinge of pain) the night Little One fell out of bed, hit his head on the corner of a lamp table and injured everyone in the house. It happened this way:

At Little One's first scream of pain, I tore out of my own bed to see what happened and jumped squarely on a scattering of metal jacks that had been missed in the nightly toy pick up. Seconds later, the children's father, jolted awake by my cries of agony, leaped from his side of the bed, gashing his shin on a Boston rocker, and fell forward, injuring the dog.

Little One's sister, owner of the lethal jacks, awoke to the wailing and crying, ran out to see what was happening and collided with the edge of her bedroom door, incurring a black eye.

A couple of hours later, we limped back to our beds wearing Band-Aids, bruises and sheepish expressions.

There were the usual encounters with toy dump trucks and tricycles left in my path and the times I nearly had my teeth knocked out wrestling a hard-headed 2-year-old into outdoor clothes. For a few years I thought about investing in steel-toed shoes to support the weight of toddlers who thought my feet were step stools.

When the children weren't setting indoor traps for us, they got us in the yard. Nothing is harder on a power mower or more deadly to humans than a tiny metal toy hidden in the grass.

"I think what I really need for mowing the lawn is a mine sweeper," said my husband one sunny Saturday morning. We were preparing to leave for the hospital emergency room, he with a cut on his forehead. Another unidentified flying object had been hidden by a child and unearthed by the power mower.

In winter they practiced germ warfare on us. They went to school and, not only picked up colds and flu, but a couple of childhood diseases neither of us had been lucky to catch before we grew up.

When we finally caught on and our injury and disease rate began dropping, they tried to cause automobile accidents. We will never forget the thrilling day when, with our car loaded with camping equipment on a busy two lane highway, a sleepy child between us kicked off the ignition. This was before the day of mandatory car seats which probably save as many parents as children.

Before I became a mother, no one ever told me that one day I'd be negotiating an icy road while trying to stop a fight between two hostile siblings and dodging their dog at the same time. All we did was slide into the ditch, but it could have been worse.

We won't even go into the bees brought into our house in a loosely capped jar, and the bees escaped and blamed me for their capture. I'll just tell you that, give or take a few scars, we made it through our children's dangerous years.

Whatever baby does, he'll do it longer than you can stand it

My mother says that the reason you don't hear many Old Wives' tales anymore is because women of today will never admit to being old wives. However I come about as close as you may get to an old wife, and what I have to say concerns your expected new baby, and what we have personally discovered.

First, the baby always wins. Someone said once that no matter what a baby does, he will do it longer than you can stand it. This is true. Arguing with a baby makes you a certain loser. Some "no nonsense" type new mothers come home from the hospital saying confidently, "I'll put him on a strict schedule right off. There's no reason why he should run our lives."

There is no reason at all except that he will. If it is his two o'clock feeding time, and he wants to sleep nothing on earth will rouse him. On the other hand if it is three o'clock and you must feed him at four you may think you win by letting him scream for an hour. But he'll make you feel so rotten mean for an hour you'll wish you'd fed him when he asked the first time.

The way you wake him up is by going to sleep yourself. Put him to sleep by planning an activity where it is necessary for him to be awake.

You can cure baby of most illnesses by immediately taking him to a pediatrician who will prescribe a $10 antibiotic. The baby will be miraculously cured while you are driving home from the drugstore. But if you do not do this right away he will fool around being sick for a week and you will still have to do it. Better go get it over with fast.

The first six cans of baby food you open will either give him a rash or be things he detests. They will mold in the refrigerator while you feel guilty about them. No, your husband cannot eat them for lunch. Moldy baby food is unfit for adult consumption.

When the baby is sleepy he will sleep. If he does not like something he will never eat it, so forget about the stuff. If he does not shut up and stop crying after fifteen minutes he may not stop until he is in the fifth grade. This is a long time to listen to a screaming kid. So pick him up. You will eventually anyway.

Mostly, if you feed him when he acts hungry, let him sleep when he acts tired, rock him when he is fussy and tell him you love him every day he will grow up to be a rather nice child who likes and trusts his parents. I know mine have. Yours will too.

Besides, any Mama who can scuba dive and knows Judo will always have respectful children.

Food Killers

Talking about children's eating habits can keep more mothers busier for longer stretches of time than hunting for Barbie doll shoes. A favorite suggestion for helping children eat has always been the idea that we "serve meals attractively."

Attractively? The average 2-year-old is indifferent to meals served in his own Donald Duck dishes or sandwiches cut in the shape of bunnies or chickies. What the toddler is most interested in at the table is making sure that his food is good and dead before he eats. And he has his own little ways of doing this.

I know of one tot I like to call The Surgeon. He operates on every morsel before he eats it, and his operations are always fatal, at least to the food. He dissects everything you put before him, removing specks of sautéed onion and green pepper, the tiniest bits of mushrooms, dabs of tomato and any lumps too small to be seen with any naked eye but his own.

When he has successfully excised all of the vital parts of his meal, he carefully shoves them off his plate and devours the remains in full view of his nauseous parents who honestly thought the kid liked macaroni casserole.

Another child assumes that food, to be fit for human consumption, must be beaten into abject submission. Using the palms of both chubby hands, he pounds and slaps his mashed potatoes, carrots and hamburger patty until they sort of lie all crushed and broken together, all of the spirit trounced out of them.

And what about the residue which has splattered on the ceiling and on Dad's trousers? Good riddance. Rebellious food that flees the plate at the first attack doesn't deserve to be eaten. It deserves to be scrapped off the floor or wherever it lands, and then thrown into the sink with the rest of the deserters.

The Mauler is another pleasant visitor, one who made our daily meals unpleasant in bygone days. The Mauler squeezes his food to death. Fistful after plump fistful is mauled, kneaded and scrunched. The only parts he considers fit to eat are those which come slurping up between his tiny fingers and onto his rosy face.

Occasionally a child will attempt to drown food before eating it by dumping a full glass of milk or orange juice over the contents of his plate, splashing it gently with his hands to make sure none of it can come up for air before he gets around to doing away with it.

Wieners and cookies quite often defeat young eaters. We find the young eater having eaten his wiener or cookie down as far as his clutched fist, screeching in anger because the rest of his goodie seems to have vanished. It is useless to attempt, at this moment, to pry open his hand. He is suffering from a hopeless condition called, "Cookie Grip."

Even if you should succeed in opening his hand, which is unlikely, his cookie will be mutilated beyond any recognition and he will scream for a fresh one.

Give it to him immediately. What's one more dead cookie compared to a house filled with peace and quiet? Also stop swearing when you clean up the mess. Do you want the kid to grow up to be a slob?

Boot camp on home front

The last time I spoke to a high school class career day about my job and we came to the question and answer session this question was asked:

"Mrs. Hansen, what in your past life prepared you to do the job you now have?"

Kids, I will not soon forget the lessons I learned during those long hard years at housework and motherhood. Nor will I cease to be grateful for the ways in which they prepared me to be a reporter.

One of those ways was never letting me stay in bed when I was sick. If my feet can move one in front of the other and I can breathe, I'll show up for work, thanks to my early training.

When you are a mother there is no such thing as too sick to get out of bed in the morning. There's dead, in which case the family does not expect you to fix the oatmeal in the morning. And then there's an occasional slight case of childbirth which is taken care of at the hospital and you are permitted to remain in bed for a bit. In between times it's you all the way, baby from 6 a.m. till midnight.

And if there is ever a major disaster here in Saginaw and they need a reporter who could get by on two hours sleep a night for a week straight, I could be their girl. Those times the babies had their days and nights mixed up prepared me for that stint.

Coping with interruptions: Fiddle-dee-dee, as Scarlett O'Hara used to say. Who does this better than former mothers of toddlers now grown to teen-hood? Back when people ironed clothes, I took pride in the fact that I could iron a shirt with an interruption every three minutes and not go insane.

Well, not entirely insane. The neighbors did used to go around saying I acted funny sometimes and there were days when I must say I felt funny, too. But I survived, didn't I?

There was this talent I have for meeting deadlines, developed over the years of having to be on time at the dentist, pediatrician and teacher's conferences. And as for being able to work under pressure:

I'll never forget that night long ago when we had just turned off the 11 o'clock news and prepared to go to bed and our son yelled down from upstairs:

"Mom, if I don't have a costume of my name saint for school tomorrow, I'll be kicked out."

St. Ralph?

You girls who've worked in offices all your lives don't know what pressure is until you've sat up until dawn making a costume for St. Ralph, of whom I had never heard of until that fateful evening when I made him up on the spot. "A saint and martyr who was burned at the stake by the Vikings in Sweden back in the fourth century."

This is the kind of creativity and working-under-pressure training that you can't beat. It might also be good for army officers going into heavy combat and substitute teachers.

Peter Rabbit required reading

Prologue from Betty: Once, when Herb and Ralph were little boys, I made them a supper of "bread and milk and blackberries", because they were "good little bunnies".

"James James Morrison Morrison Weatherby George Dupree took great care of his mother though he was only three."

Once I was the only woman in the neighborhood who knew volumes of Christopher Robin poems by heart. Others could quote T.S. Elliot and wonder if a dirty book like Ulysses could every get printed in the United States. But I read only to my children. Other women knew what funny Dorothy Parker said. The only humorous remark I knew about was the one Little Black Sambo made when the tiger told him he couldn't wear Black Sambo's littler purple shoes on his four big paws.

I remember when an old friend I hadn't seen in years asked me what I'd been reading lately. "Well, right now, 'The Little Pink House on the Hill', and I'm half way through 'Millions of Cats,'" I replied, thinking she meant what was I reading lately and the only reading I'd been doing lately was to the kids. "Oh Betty, you are always the funniest girl." she giggled and went around for days telling everyone what a wit I was. She never dreamed I was telling the truth.

It wasn't the simplicity of children's literature I minded. After being up all night with a baby, Basic English is about all anyone can manage. What I minded was the deadly, killing maddening repetition. A child's taste in reading never runs to variety. If he likes Peter Rabbit he likes Peter Rabbit for months. And just about the time his mother gets so she can recite, "When 'round the end of a cucumber frame whom should he first meet but Mr. McGregor," while simultaneously planning meals and balancing her checkbook, her little listener will remark, "I don't like that story anymore. Find me a new one."

Another thing I minded about reading to children was that nothing could ever be abridged. Once a child has heard a story you can never change a word. It can be 9 P.M., guest waiting downstairs for cards and drinks, but do you dare leave out one conversation with a lousy tiger or skip one of the three nasty little pigs? Never. In fact, you can't even skip periods or commas. But I told myself it was worthwhile if my children grew up with a love of good books and reading. I'm not really sure they did.

Then came the evening when the adult conversation turned to gourmet food and great restaurants. They spoke of the chicken Kiev here and the oefs' en gelee someplace else. Did you ever sit in on talk like this and realize that if you don't contribute fast it will be too late and you will be thought an imbecile forever? "But, Flopsy, Mopsy and Cottontail, who were good little bunnies, had bread and milk and blackberries for supper," said I gaily quoting the only thing about food that popped into my mind.

"Oh, I say, that's rich" said the gentleman next to me. (Don't you just hate people who say, "That's rich", or "beautiful" instead of laughing like mad when they think you are funny? "May I use that someday?"

"Go right ahead," I shrugged. "It's only a little quotation from Peter Rabbit, and if old Pete doesn't mind, I'm sure I don't."

And as A.A. Milne put it, "James James said to his mother, 'Mother' he said, said he, "You must never go down to the end of the town, if you don't go down with me." It was a good number of years before I was able to do this little thing.

Children Not Just Raised; They Just Survive

It occurred to me the other day that we are not going to the doctor's office as often as we did a few years ago. When we began raising our family we embarked upon what we now refer to as the Era of the Pediatrician. It started innocently enough with the dumb little things like my not knowing how to adjust the baby's formula and proceeded from sniffles and fussiness to measles, mumps and chicken pox. Then there were allergies, infections, viruses and Lord knows what.

Anyway, what with having a baby every other year it got so our weekly visit to the pediatrician was a regular event. It we missed a week, the doctor called to find out why - which is more than we could say for our pastor. But everyone said, "Don't worry, when they get older and going to school this sort of thing passes."

It is possible that "everyone" did not have four boys in a row. For when they started school they really started living big. Talk about battered children. For years these kids fell out of trees, ran headlong into brick walls and got hit over the head by other kids. They fell off their bikes, stopped baseballs, golf balls and defensive halfbacks. They waded into fishing ponds and nearly bled to death from cuts from hidden glass. The staff in the hospital emergency room and I soon got on a first name basis and there was some talk of naming a memorial emergency booth for us.

There was also some talk about our being investigated by Blue Cross. They just couldn't believe it. Then we had a little girl, a dainty curly-haired, brown-eyed little beauty who looked as if she stepped straight from a Victorian painting. "Everyone" earnestly assured me that "girls are so much different." When she was nine she was treated on three successive weeks for swimmer's ear, a head injury from a golf club swung by a playmate and landing on a rusty nail while playing Superman.

But the three older boys grew up, went to college and grew beards, and were certified 1-A by the United States Armed Forces. Evidently the girls are all going to live too. And from all of this we have been able to draw one conclusion and it is this: By and large, children are not really raised, they just survive.

What is Home Without 'Mom?'

Whoever writes the headlines for my column at the Saginaw News seems rather fond of calling me "Mom." I kind of like it, even though it does sound like the rock and roll ballad where the teenager "just can't tell his mom cause she just ain't got the time." Well, that sounds familiar anyway, even if my children do not know that when The News says "Mom" it's me they're talking about.

Around home everyone calls me "Ma." It bothers me a little. I don't know how it ever got started. But somehow the image is wrong. The mother of the Barker-Karpis mob was also called Ma, as was the matriarch of the Kettle Clan. But honestly, have you ever heard of anyone calling Rose Kennedy or Queen Elizabeth "Ma"? See what I mean by image?

Lots of mothers are called "Mama." You really should be fat to carry this off well. Maybe I should gain some weight. And little girls in TV commercials all say "Mommy", which sounds cute if "Mommy" is young and also a model. It gets a little sticky if Mommy is pushing 59.

In some circles it is considered chic for children to address their mothers by their given names, particularly if it is something stylish like Pamela or Liz. But there is something deep inside me which rebels at getting this chummy with the kids. It's tough enough keeping order around here without the children getting me confused with the babysitter. And somehow "Hey Betty, where are my shorts?" just doesn't sound right coming from a 16-year-old son.

Victorian kiddies called their female parent, "Ma-ma" with the accent on the last syllable, if we are to believe movies about Victorian kiddies. And it used to be that you could tell the Englishman in a play right off by the way he called his mother "Matter."

I call my mother "Mother". Personally I think it has a nice sound, and reminds me of Whistler, Irish ballads and pink carnations. Mother may kill me for this, since she is blonde, has published a couple of books and is a "swinger" in Largo, FL., where she is supposed to be "retired".

I hope someone calls me "Mother" someday. I can just see me in my sunset years, with a black silk dress and white pompadour, leaning on my cane with matriarchal majesty. But you can just bet anything that some dumb kid will ruin the whole effect by yelling, "Hey Ma, when do we eat?"

Mom Expert on Meaning of Stress 1967

Dawn breaks around our house like a 21-gun salute. The other day I read that some scientists are studying the effects of "stress" upon human beings. It's odd that they have not approached me about this, because when I talk of stress, I speak as an expert.

Do you know what stress is? It is ironing five children out of the house on a cold winter morning, simultaneously fixing six things for breakfast, packing lunches, finding mittens, and in the midst of the confusion hearing a seventh-grader wail for help with a lesson.

It is cleaning up the house Monday after Sunday when the place looks like a Roman arena after all the gladiators stayed to dinner. It is having to go to a luncheon when you don't feel like it. But the bearing of the person who asked you is so commanding that you know who is running the PTA.

Stress is driving to school in the pouring rain to pick up your poor tired athlete after the football practice and discovering that he has offered rides to nine other poor tired little athletes, none under six feet tall or 190 pounds. It is sitting at a high school game feeling dreadful when your son is sitting on the bench and worse when he starts to play.

Stress is folding laundry. It is packing for vacations, standing in supermarket lines, shopping for Christmas and Easter and getting ready for a party. Stress is having a son too young and inexperienced to handle a brand new baby but too old to be left with the teen-age girl you have hired as a babysitter. It is the shock of discovering that the only good pair of nylons in the house is being worn by your daughter.

Stress is holding back tears when your child has the honor of delivering his graduating class and saying good-bye when he leaves for the service. It is waiting for a daughter to have a baby of her own. And it is hoping every day that each one you love will grow up to be loved by someone else and that each will find his heart's desire, whatever that is.

When you stop to think of it, isn't this kind of stress wonderful? Truly, I don't believe I would trade my own hectic stressful life for anything. How about you?

Moms must keep cool

"How do you manage to stay so calm so much of the time?" someone asked me. Truthfully, I was not always thus. It's what has happened over a long and lively life that got me in this calm condition.

Somewhere along the way I discovered that a crisis only lasts long enough to be crucial and in most cases one is a survivor. If a crisis lasts long enough it becomes a way of life and a person can still emerge a survivor.

I think I first learned the value of external self-control when our Ralph was five years old, and I was expecting a baby. I was lying on the bed worrying over my pregnancy and my thyroid condition when he came in from play with a raging fever. Maybe it's only the flu, I thought hopefully. It turned out he had polio.

Nobody in the family ever caught cold or German measles or something simple. They went in for grand diseases. Once two of them had infectious hepatitis at the same time and once when I was about to go to the hospital myself three of them came down with the measles.

A mother of a large family develops reflexes like a cat so that she can, and I did, simultaneously make a batch of strawberry jam, catch a child toppling from a cupboard, and stop the water from running over in the bathroom without even losing track of her labor pains. So don't talk to me about calm. I learned it the hard way.

If I could think of any quality conductive to excellent mental health in a mother, it is absolute, unshakeable, unflappable, rise-to-any-occasion-in-the-world type of cool. This is the mother who daily pulls into the school driveway with a station wagon full of 16 second graders. How else do you think she got there alive?

I admire a woman who can serenely face three months of getting up in the night to feed a colicky baby, or a wet two-year-old without being reduced to an angry, spanking, shrieking witch. If little troubles like this get you down wait until the big ones get here.

I don't think I every fully realized this until the birth of our severely retarded child when we had to learn to live with conditions I would have thought impossible before. And even now when the going gets tough I remind myself that people have survived concentration camps, bombings, and poverty and my own personal crisis reduces itself considerably.

When a couple of readers took me to task for saying that as a child I believed in God, a Santa Clause type of deity who gave me everything I asked for, I had to smile a little. Certainly I still believed in God, but he is not the same one I knew as a child.

The god I know as a grown-up is one whom I am sure through these years of raising my family has been carrying at least half my daily load. Because if He hadn't been, I could never have maintained one half the calm I am told I have.

My personal argument for anyone developing a serene and accepting attitude toward most of the problems of living is that the sea of life is storm tossed and trouble enough without being stupid enough to rock one's own boat.

And while it is right for us to shower God with thanks for our many blessings it is also a find idea to accept the troubles he sends us with as much good grace and equanimity as we can muster. We owe Him this much anyway.

Sandbox Saga

Now that I think about I, it was a good thing that we weren't expected to think metric that time I ordered the sand for the children's sandbox.

They were young enough for sandboxes then, and while they built sand castles and roads, I sat on the porch reading numerous magazine articles on how I should keep all of the responsibilities of housework and child care a secret from my hard working husband.

The idea then was that a good wife never bothered her busy husband with the horrid, nit-picking details of her own day. After all wasn't he out there in the jungle, trying to be a success? If the children were to appear in court for stealing hub caps, he must never know.

They never did, of course, but even if they had, I wouldn't have told him. Did the house burn down? Unless you would ruin him or see him have a heart attack, it was your job as a good wife to rebuild it quickly so he could come home to a smoothly running household. They assumed husbands either traveled for years on end or put in a lot of overtime.

But this is what housewives were told back in 1959 when my children still played in sandboxes and thinking was reserved for men. And it brings us right back to the day I filled the sandbox, or had it filled, without asking my husband's help, thereby freeing him of the responsibilities of home and family.

At the time we had five little responsibilities in the family, all of them his fault. But still, why should I bother him with a little thing like sand for the children. True, he had promised to drive out to the sandpits some Sunday and bring back a couple of bushels of sand. But I didn't want him to have heart attack doing it, did I?

Women's magazines were filled with advice on how to keep our husbands from having heart attacks, little suggestions like killing yourself by putting on your own garage roof, stuff like that. You'd be dead of strain, but you would have died knowing you spared your husband.

I said this to myself as I looked up the number of the sand and gravel company. And I even said it without laughing because that is what we really believed in those days.

"How do you sell sand?" I asked.

"By the yard," was the astonishing reply of the man on the other end of the phone.

I had this mental picture of sand coming in bushel baskets or small dump trucks. The image of sand being measured out like dress goods confused me.

"We don't deliver less than five yards either," said the man.

Five yards of dress goods mad a dress. It didn't sound like much and I could hardly blame him for not wanting to deliver such a pitiful little bit of sand.

"I'll have seven yards," I said magnanimously so he wouldn't think I was cheap.

"You're sure?"

"Absolutely. I wouldn't take a foot less."

Never having seen seven yards of sand I had no idea how magnanimous I was until the mountain was dumped in my driveway. I had intended to have it put in the sandbox, but I forgot about the yard fence.

My five little responsibilities clambered around Sand Mountain which was quickly becoming a neighborhood landmark. Their friends climbed with them making envious noises. No other kids had an eight-foot-high hill blocking the driveway.

It was now 4:45. I had yet to fix my nutritious, attractive evening meal, dress the children and myself in our dinnertime best and mix up the required cold drink so my husband could relax when he came in from the industrial jungle. If, I reflected, I could do all this and move Sand Mountain elsewhere by 5:30 p.m. they'd write me up in Ladies Home Journal for sure.

On the other hand, I realized the attempt might also get me written up in some other kind of journal. Clearly, Sand Mountain was the kind of project that would take real teamwork. I went into the house, tossed some wieners into a pan of boiling water and mixed myself a cold drink so I could relax.

Frankly, I reasoned probably a glimmering of the first liberated thought I ever had if it hadn't been for him and our five little responsibilities I would never have needed sand in the first place.

Anyway, by midnight we had filled our sandbox and every other sandbox for miles around, made several deals for the removal of the rest of the sand, consumed a number of cold, relaxing drinks and were well into a discussion of who got custody of the children after the divorce.

That was fifteen years ago and we are still together, partly because we couldn't agree on who had to have custody of the children. Also, it took a while to dispose of the seven yards of sand. And I suppose you are looking for some point to all of this.

Actually there isn't one. Except that when I was young and unliberated, too few girls went into marriage knowing that a yard of sand wasn't the same as a yard of cloth. There were a lot of other things we didn't know besides. It made the difference.

The crabbiest teacher in school

Miss Jones was a "crabby" teacher. Years ago a small boy sat in our kitchen, eating cookies and worrying.

"Boy, I'm really going to hate school this year. All the guys say Miss Jones is the crabbiest teacher in school."

"Why don't you wait and see?" I suggested. "You might find out she is quite nice."

"Yeah? Well, the kids who had her know how mean she is." He finished his cookies and wandered outdoors to worry some more about crabby Miss Jones. Through the entire month of August, stories of Miss Jones' cruelty to children filled our family conversations. Even I began to wonder about her a little.

September came and the first week of school. Our small boy didn't have much to say about Miss Jones or his day-to-day encounters with her crabbiness.

One night he brought home some spelling papers. He had been instructed to do them over. They were very messy, Miss Jones had told him. I quite agreed.

"Miss Jones says if it isn't our very best work, we shouldn't bother handing it in. She'll kill us if she sees messy papers."

The picture of Miss Jones, surrounded by killed students was too much. I left my son to his work copying his spelling lists.

He took to scrubbing his hands and face with extra care at night. "Miss Jones can't stand dirty kids. She even makes us wash after recess. And you know how crabby she is!"

We said we'd heard and watched him brush his hair each morning. Miss Jones also didn't like sloppy looking boys.

He began bringing home books from the library – every week another book to be read and reported upon in the classroom.

"You know what crabby old Jonesy would do if we didn't read all the time," he reminded us. She'd kill him, of course. It was clear that pleasing Miss Jones was a matter of survival.

I met Miss Jones at the first PTA meeting of the year. Slender, white-haired and awesomely aristocratic, I could see where she impressed my son and his classmates. I was impressed.

"Your boy had a fine mind and a lot of potential," she said. "I intend to see that he lives up to both of them." This was no less than a pronouncement   of a queen of the realm.

Years later, I met Miss Jones again, this time on the street. She had retired, but looked no different than she looked when I first saw her. We talked about the small boy we had both known so well.

"He's in college now, on the Dean's List," I told her proudly.

"I knew he would be," said Miss Jones, "All he needed to do was learn to apply himself and give nothing but his best."

We chatted. I was pleased and flattered that she remembered so many little things about him, things I had forgotten.

"I remember your boy well," she said walking away. "I remember all of them." A teardrop clung to the corner of her eye as we said goodbye. I promised I would tell my son we had met again.

Only yesterday, the small daughter of the boy now grown up came to visit with her parents.

"I hope we move before school starts next year," she told me. "All the kids say Miss Smith is the crabbiest teacher in the school."

I hugged her and smiled.

"I hope so dear. Oh, I do hope she is.

Emergency Room is a fashion disaster area

"It wasn't bad enough that she had to have three stitches in her lip when she fell off the kitchen stool," lamented my young friend up the street. "But I had to rush her to the emergency room with my hair in rollers and wearing that duster that I have to pin up the front."

We were talking about another of "Hansen's Laws" governing the management of a household, this time the one that says, "A kid's chances of having to be rushed to the emergency room are in direct proportion to how bad his mother looks at that moment."

Only a mother who once drove a son with a broken leg to the hospital barefoot and wearing her husband's painting clothes could know how it feels. I have a theory about pictures I see supposedly of deprived people of Appalachia lined up waiting for help in the welfare office.

In reality they are middle class parents who have had to rush children to the emergency room for everything from cut lips on the 3-year-olds to broken noses 16-year-old football players.

That man sitting there with his pants on backwards, wearing his wife's blouse, was taking a nap when his daughter fell off her tricycle. His wife? Oh, this was her Saturday morning bowling outing.

The girl next to him, the one whose 6-year-old got a black eye from the neighborhood bully...probably the hospital staff will believe forever that she goes around with dripping wet hair and a towel around her neck.

The nurses and doctors in the emergency wing are clustered around the desks, probably engaged in all sorts of heavy dramatic stuff, the way they do in General Hospital.

It's hard to interrupt them, trying to look cool with your stomach wet from hand washing sweaters, wearing an old army raincoat, to help them take care of your child's bloody nose, most of which is on you by now.

There is another side to the prevention of minor family accidents. Stay dressed up when boys are at football practice. It even helps to be nearly dressed for their basketball stints. One never knows.

Wear shoes when they go out to ride their tricycles. Comb your hair in the morning, if it isn't too much trouble. And nap with your clothes on. You never know when somebody is going to fall out of the crib.

Thumb-suckers: long may they slurp

It's been a long time since I sucked my thumb - say about half a century. Still, I'm no less delighted to learn that thumb-sucking by babies is now considered, not merely acceptable, but a habit to be warmly encouraged.

This piece of great good news comes from no less an expert on child care than Dr. T. Berry Brazelton, professor at Harvard Medical School. I'm only sorry he couldn't have said it sooner.

How well I remember the very first child of mine was caught sucking his thumb. I must say that I am not the one who caught him in this evil deed, mostly because I'd seen him doing it almost from birth and thought it was something all babies did.

It was my mother-in-law, who, peeking into his little bassinet, let out a gasp of horror and whispered, "Thumb sucking is a nasty habit which must be broken at all costs," and she went home and made him a pair of thumbless mittens to see that it was.

I was given to understand that as a pass-time, thumb-sucking ranked with another unmentionable habit once said to cause small boys to go blind. I mention this only to give you some idea of how thumb-sucking was regarded at that particular time.

It was an era when anything which might make a baby content was regarded as unhealthy if not wicked. We're nicer to babies now. Spock may have caused a few kids to decide to be hippies, but he never insisted you keep infants in a state of misery.

But back to Dr. Brazelton and his bold advocacy of thumb-sucking. I was way ahead of him, I'm proud to say. It didn't take but a baby or two for me to discover that thumb-in-mouth cherubs were superior as companions to babies who yelled all the time.

Ignoring my mother-in-law's dire warnings, I became one of the biggest thumb pushers in the country. "You feeling miserable kid? I know just the thing to fix you up. Try sucking your thumb for a while. It won't cost you a thing but a dirty look from your grandmother.

Along with thumb-sucking my young picked up another bad habit. (These things never come to you singly, you know.) That bad habit was known as "The Blankie." A child with a blankie can change a family's entire scheme of existence.

Fortunate are the parents whose child accompanies his thumb-sucking by twirling a lock of his own hair. Not so lucky are those whose tots' security depends on a ragged old blanket they've known since day five, or whenever they first came home from the hospital.

I've always thought babies should be born with blankies attached to them someplace which naturally would fall off when the kid stops sucking his thumb. You'd save a lot of time that way. As attached as babies are to blankies they manage to mislay them a million times a day and depend upon their parents to keep track of them.

So much for babies, blankies, thumbs and pediatrics. It was nice of Dr. Brazelton to come out the way he did for thumb-sucking. He's a real pioneer. Just in time for the grandchildren, too.

Memory of youngsters' firsts lasts a long time

Among the numberless joys of having grown-up children is knowing they are all potty trained. One wonders how, sometimes. I look back on that period of my life (and theirs) as a time of complete abject failure. Potty training toddlers was a task I did not accomplish with any degree of skill or class. I sort of muddled through until they figured out the idea for themselves.

Even now, it's impossible not to be awed by efficient jewels of motherhood whose youngsters are in training pants by six months and completely house broken at one year. There should be some kind of a day in their honor.

"I haven't washed a diaper in six months," used to be the smug boast among these jewels. Now the phrase has been updated: "We haven't bought a box of Pampers since little Max was 10 months old."

In either era I was at the bottom of the class, so to speak. Even our infrequent puppies defied me, knowing right off they'd lucked out and found themselves in the house of a non-housebreaker.

But although the potty-training years of motherhood were not among my best, due to a solemn pact the children made with each other in their cribs to make me look bad at all costs, they were not without some achievements. I could have bragged too.

I could have bragged how they were the first in the neighborhood to crawl out of their cribs and into the lipstick drawer.

They were the first to figure out how the lock on the screen door worked, first to escape, first to lose their shoes on Sunday morning as we dressed for church and first to slam their own fingers in a door.

One of them achieved the honor of being first to say a naughty word most currently being bandied about the sandbox crowd, plainly enough to be understood by every adult in hearing distance.

They were the first to play doctor, first to knock someone off a tricycle, first to visit the emergency room and first to discover that if you fiddle with a phone long enough, you can call the Bangkok Embassy direct.

So you can see, I wasn't without my share of "my kid was the first one in the neighborhood to..." stories to tell. The problem was that a lot of their firsts were not things I cared to brag about.

Snow day: Lord's gift to good kids, bad moms

Last week in our village we had what officials call "a snow day." When I was in school, lacking conciseness of modern day education relations men, we call it, "that day it snowed so hard they closed the schools." Our parents called it other foul and obscene things.

For the benefit of those who cannot remember, a snow day is when the superintendent of schools looks out his bedroom window and, with the help of his wife, the Lord and the lady who drives Bus 22, (on the phone, of course) decides that roads and weather are too rotten to have school.

When I was a little girl I thought snow days came because I had been good. In the words of the "I'm OK, You're OK" crowd, I looked upon our very rare snow days as a stroke from the Almighty.

I'd lace my legs into my brown leather girls' high-topped boots, put on a pair of my brother's corduroy knickers and run out-doors to wallow in the wonderful, cold white stuff that kept the school closed that day.

I supposed that my teacher, Old Lady McGillicuddy, was home gnashing her teeth in helpless rage because school was closed and she couldn't get me for a whole day. At that time I also supposed this was the only pleasure in life Old Lady McGillicuddy had.

How was I to know that Miss McGillicuddy was home making a fresh pot of coffee and thinking thankful thoughts like, "No more pencils, no more books, no more kids with stupid looks, at least not for today."

It wasn't until I grew up to be a mother that I discovered the other side of snow days and formed the opinion that God sent snow days because I had been bad. He didn't exactly strike me with lightening, the way my preacher relatives had said He would.

Instead he dumped several thousand tons of snow on the town so I couldn't send the kids to school and go back to bed. It was then it also occurred to me that perhaps Old Lady McGillicuddy was not quite as enraged by snow days as I had believed in my childhood.

My friend looked out the window as the first snowflake drifted to the ground. "Oh, I hope we have a snow day tomorrow. I need Connie and Cathy home to help me make cookies."

"You wouldn't do a thing to me like wish for a snow day," I cried incredulously. "I've got all these kids who will make 500 trips in and out of the house all day, tracking snow, and they'll each have three friends with them whose mothers have locked them out of the house for the day."

"Pray for a snow day," my child orders his siblings, on viewing that same snowflake.

"Please God; I've been good all year. I even cleaned the stove. Don't send a snow day," pleads his mother, as the first snowflake turns into the Great Snowstorm of '73.

Across the village Old Lady McGillicuddy's nephew, who is not superintendent of schools, looks out his bedroom window and, with the help his wife, the Lord and the lady who drives Bus 22, ponders our fate, for the coming day.

Rainy Saturday Traumatic Togetherness

Between rainy Saturdays I tend to forget about them. I suppose that is because this is because, as psychologists tell us, we blot traumatic experiences from our memory. And rainy Saturday's around "Old House" are traumatic to over use a word.

Rainy Saturday is when the same rotten kid who must be dragged from his bed at 7:45 on school days, arises at 6 a.m. to call all of his friends on the phone. "But how come they aren't up yet? Its morning, isn't it?"

Rainy Saturday is the day we are visited promptly at 8 a.m. by the children of all the immaculate housekeepers in the neighborhood. "Can I play in your house today? My mother is getting ready for her bridge club."

"We have to play here today. Mama doesn't want our house mussed up and we give her a headache if we stay in on Saturday."

"Bobby can't play at our house today. It's raining and mama doesn't want the neighbor kids tracking in mud so she sent us over here."

While the children of immaculate housekeepers are upstairs turning out the dresser drawers and dancing on the beds, we have some children of our own who literally don't know enough to come in out of the rain. What they don't understand is that you can only play in the pouring rain so long and you get wet...sopping, muddy wet.

Their Rainy Saturday is spend going outdoors, coming in, stripping to the buff and looking for dry things so they can go back outside. Between hunting through the laundry for clean socks and waiting for the dryer to shut off, this group of kids rarely gets further than the back hall.

Also on Rainy Saturday we have football games in the recreation room...on television. These games attract a gang of extremely large high school boys who sit all afternoon in their damp jackets looking as if they were going to leave any minute. I worry about them, but they seem to stay healthy.

And in the midst of all this togetherness is sure to be one bored individual who wanders around sucking his thumb and insisting there is no one to play with. He is unaware that every child within a radius of six blocks is in his house, practically knocking him down on the way to the bathroom.

As you have guessed another Rainy Saturday has come and gone and we have survived, just as Jon Hall and Dorothy Lamoure used to survive the typhoons in the South Sea movies. Only don't talk to me for a while about the joys of motherhood or tell me that this is the best time of my life. In fact, don't talk to me at all for about a week and if it doesn't rain again next Saturday maybe I'll have something pleasant to say.

Tot's first bad word a shocker

You'd think the way colorful language is now tossed about socially, what my kids used to call, "bad words" would no longer shock parents. It turns out this is not true.

A child's first socially unacceptable word reverberates across a crowded room like a gunshot. Maybe I'm overly sensitive about this, having raised mostly boys, but you can bet your copy of Ginott that the first kid in the tot lot to cuss will be a boy.

My sons made it a point to utter their first naughty words either in the hearing of a little old lady up the street or the nice little girl whose mother swore (on Bibles) that no one at THEIR house EVER talked like that.

It's like I told the little old lady up the street when she phoned in a complaint about the nasty language used by the 10-year-old and his gang:

"I don't even think those words, let alone use them when I drop the frying pan on my foot at 7 in the morning.

But as she told me, "Children hear that in the home. You'll never convince me otherwise." I hung up the phone, knowing it was useless to try.

As it happened, the 10-year-old hadn't used the words I used when I dropped the skillet on my foot. Those words were, I'll admit, colorful, but not obscene.

Oddly enough he also didn't repeat the word his father used the day we were driving along the expressway and the baby nosedived off my lap to retrieve her Popsicle which had dropped on his foot – the one he had pressed on the gas pedal.

You get grateful for small blessings.

For those whose children have not yet learned to talk, let me tell you about your child's first bad word. And he will say it.

Furthermore, having discovered a word that can reduce adults to silence, produce gasps (however phony) from bystanders and throw his parents into shock. Easy Cusser is not going to perform without an audience.

Your child guidance book will tell you the best procedure is to ignore it. Go ahead, if you think you can. But let me ask you: Have you ever ignored your roof blowing off your house or paid no attention to the semi which has just driven through your living room wall? Have you pretended not to notice that there is a 25-foot-tall archangel standing at your side looking on in disapproval?

This is how hard it is to ignore your child's first bad word, publicly spoken. His (by now) vast audience of disapproving listeners is waiting impatiently for you to do something constructive – say like washing his mouth out with soap. They don't care what your baby book says. They want vengeance.

And everyone present knows why you are ignoring Easy Cusser. It's not because your baby book said to, it's because privately you talk like a dock hand yourself. Ask any disapproving face present. As the pediatrician-author of "How to Grow Up Children at Home in Your Spare Time" puts it, "My view is, no dammed kid of mine is going to use bad words." What you have to do to survive is develop proper attitude.

A child's creative vocabulary matures too soon

To one who has just blown out three candles on a pink-frosted birthday cake, the miracle of spoken words is still unsullied by a need to speak them, according to grammarians.

"I'll have a whole full of it," my child announced, holding up an empty bowl. There was no need to explain to me, her mother, that I'd better be generous with her favorite dessert. Even her term for her favorite dessert was a perfect description of what she wanted.

When you are 3 and you don't want bananas or fruit cocktail in your jello, what do you ask for? You ask for a bowl of "empty" jello, naturally. This daughter is grown up now and the teachers charged with instructing her to speak and write correctly have done an excellent job. But you don't know too many words at age 3 and therefore, it is necessary to be very creative with the ones you do know in order to be understood.

Just this morning I was thinking about the creativity and poetry of small children's speech with more than a touch of nostalgia. How often in a lifetime does one hear such a vivid assessment of the difference between grownups and little people as I did on the day she woefully pointed out I was "way up to the high," and she was "way down to the little." I was, therefore, much better equipped to get her favorite toy down from a top shelf of a bookcase.

For nearly a year she kept up her poetic license with words which, by then, were filling her mind almost faster than she could assimilate them. "It's darking out," she observed one late summer afternoon as thunderstorm clouds turned the sunny skies into an early dusk.

I used to listen, fascinated, as she combined two words with such perfect logic.

"Everyone went to the show 'butcept' daddy," she noticed one Saturday on the way home from the movies.

"Mom," she complained, from her crowded spot on the living room couch, "makin him move over, he's 'squishing' me." It's tough, I agreed, being so small and being squished between two older brothers who fail to make room. Everyone in the family liked this brand new verb and it became a household word for squeezed, crushed or crowded -- take your choice.

Watching me dish up mashed potatoes she made sure she'd get enough of one of her favorite foods. "I'll have two glumps of them," she announced at dinner. Well, anybody in a right mind knows immediately what a glump of mashed potatoes is. It's that amount that you scoop onto the serving spoon and "glump" down on the plate. For two glumps, you glumped twice.

On windy days the wind "pushed" her and laughing with excitement she pushed back. Sometimes the weather was not so good. Its "glummy outside," she announced, pressing her nose against a window with rain streaming down the other side.

She had a Barbie doll with "squirmally" arms and another doll with a "falls-off" head, and an endless vocabulary of descriptive words no one had ever used before or have used since. Once she visited "daddy's work" and was terrified by the loud noises in the plant. For a long time afterward she referred to the place as the "Scaring Gear."

I never corrected her taking as much pleasure as I could in her special and rapidly disappearing language. In my opinion, we start too soon to stamp out creativity and original thinking in youngsters and replace it with what we oldsters deem "proper."

Before I barely had a chance to commit her special secret language to memory, she'd learned enough words to replace it herself. The language was left behind along with the doll with the squirmally arms and pushy autumn winds. But her language didn't die forever, I'm pleased to announce. Once in a while a word or two surfaces in conversations with my smallest grandchildren.

It's pleasant to recall again the freshness a beginning talker gives to our tired old way of conversation, even if it's just for a little while.

Endless Era: Tooth Fairy Years

The longest years of motherhood could be The Tooth Fairy years. When God created babies I think He decided there'd never be enough time to get their teeth all worked out before they were born, so He left Tooth Fairy time to their mothers.

True, some children lose baby teeth gracefully, the same way they didn't break out in a rash the minute they came home from the hospital as infants. They are the same tots who started right out sleeping all night and not crying around grandparents.

But there are other children (mine mostly) who faced losing a tooth the way grown-ups would anticipate losing an arm or a leg. Luckily they only lose them one at a time. Frankly, I gave birth with less fuss than my children lost their baby teeth.

A child's tooth isn't much larger than a crumb. When it is loose it appears to be attached to the mouth by the kind of wire that is said to be strong enough to lift a Chevrolet. The impending loss of this tooth is heralded with a glad cry, or maybe it is only a cry:

"Mama, my tooth is loose, feel," presenting a wet mouth filled with baby teeth and partly dissolved sucker. If there is anything on earth I can't abide, next to a warmed-up chair in a doctor's office, it is sticking my finger in a child's mouth. I know there are lots of mothers in the world who do not find this nauseating, maybe that's why I have always been a failure, mother-wise. I can't give pills to dogs either. And I could never have been a dentist. Anyway, enough of my feelings about sticking my finger in someone else's mouth. This doesn't mean I never have. By shutting my eyes, concentrating on happy thoughts and swallowing hard I have managed to feel literally hundreds of loose teeth, sometimes as often as every 10 minutes in an average 18-hour day.

Of course, by this time the loose tooth is driving the whole family a little batty, what with having to feel it and hear about it for hours on end. And by now it dangles from a thread of that wire guaranteed strong enough to lift a Chevrolet, and you wonder if this isn't' where the wire came from originally.

"Just loop a piece of string around it and give it a good yank," is grandma's advice. Of course, like much of grandma's advice this direction has its basis in myth, not fact.

String is too bulky to wrap around a crumb size tooth. On the other hand, have you ever tried to lasso a crumb size tooth with a sodden loop of number 40 white thread?

A courageous, but dishonest and desperate mother can say to her child, "Let me see how loose it really is," grasp the slippery, tiny item as firmly as possible and yank. If she is lucky she will extract the offending tooth to the indignant cries of her child, "You promised me you wouldn't pull it."

If she is even luckier, the wire strong enough to lift a Chevrolet will hold firm and the youngster, once he has stopped screaming that she tried to kill him, will never again ask his treacherous parent to feel in his mouth for his loose tooth. Finally, if she is very, very lucky, the tooth will fall out someplace else all by itself, and all she will have to put up with then are the sobs and trauma when it is discovered that half a glass of water she dumped down the sink contained the crumb size tooth waiting for the Tooth Fairy.

I hate the little nerd - said the rivalrous sibling

When I was a little kid, I hated my brother. I really detested the little creep. It wasn't until he grew up that I discovered he had some really fine qualities I'd been missing all those childhood years when I plotted his end.

This is called "sibling rivalry" by child psychologists. "Who the heck brought that screamy little kid into the house, and get him out of here quick, before I squash him."

Knowing all this, and keeping my own relationship with my brother firmly in mind, I was not surprised to find the condition in full bloom, or full fester, if you will, as my own children began "welcoming" new arrivals into the home.

I've come to the conclusion as a result, that there is no such thing as brotherly love. It was something invented by Adam and Eve, after Cain and Abel had their big blow up, to keep other brothers and sisters from doing each other in.

I had this friend once who, before her second child was born, vowed she'd fight brother-sister jealousy all the way, beginning while the sibling was still in the womb.

"I've got it all figured out," she said smugly. "The book says I should let Terry feel responsible for the baby. So I tell him this is HIS baby." She smiled at me, still looking like the cat who ate the canary.

Well, if there's anything I can't stand its people who come up with stupid ideas like this and act as if they'd been touched with divine wisdom or something. And I'd already been through the sibling rivalry thing two or three times myself, which didn't touch me with divine wisdom so much as with earthly cynicism. So I said:

"Go ahead. And when you bring the baby home and you want to feed him, but Terry thinks it's his baby and wants to punch him in the stomach, you'll smile out of the other side of your face."

Somebody wise – I think it was Dr. Spock or one of his colleagues – once asked,

"How would you like it if your husband brought home another much younger woman and said, 'This is the new addition to our family. She's going to live with us and share your room, your things and also my affection. And I'm sure you'll love her as much as I do.'"

And you'd say to yourself, if indeed you did say it quietly to yourself, which I doubt, "Ha, that's all you know. I'll get rid of that rotten intruder if it's the last thing I do." And then you'd do it. Only it wouldn't be the last thing you'd do, it'd be the next thing.

And if your husband was dumb enough to say this new person in your house was yours, you know how fast you'd get rid of her. And this is what sibling rivalry is all about.

But grandmas still insist on telling an enraged and jealous 3-year-old, "Nonsense, you LOVE your baby sister. Everyone loves his baby sister. What's wrong with you, Kid, anyway?"

And we all go around thinking, "Yeah, what IS wrong with me? I can't stand the little nerd, how come everyone else in the family thinks she's so great?"

All of this is by the way of telling you about the latest sibling rivalry crisis at our house which involves an old car shared by the two youngest. The use if for getting back and forth to school, going to practice, dates and trips to the store.

I know about the two mothers to whom Solomon suggested they cut the baby in half and share it equally, and the real mother spoke up and said, "You don't have to go that far, she can keep the kid, for all of me."

But if I said, "Why not chop the car in half and share it equally, do you think that would settle anything?" All the two rightful owners of the car would say was, "Boy, Mom, you always were some kind of screwball."

Is there such a thing as terminal sibling rivalry?

Mom, Dad always have money? Non-cents

Parents caught up in the current financial squeeze ought to take a lesson from their grandparents who learned early in the Great Depression that children are a big fat leak in the pocketbook. It's a leak overlooked in most of the advice published on how to stay afloat on a singing economic ship.

My dad could tell them a thing or two. In spite of the fact that we employed a maid and drove around in a Packard sedan, he had all of us kids convinced we were poor. If we asked him for a penny reward for going to the store, it was alike asking for a trip down the cold, dark road to the poorhouse.

This was, of course, when the corner grocery store operated as an annex to the pantry to the people who lived within walking distance. If you ran out of something you send one of the children for it -- on foot -- none of this driving two blocks for a loaf of bread.

There was nothing wrong with paying a kid for doing this, provided the kid knew it was payment for a job done and not just a penny carelessly tossed out to the undeserving.

It was a cold war against prosperity -- a war of think rich, talk poor. It also was a propaganda scheme used by Depression parents to prevent their young from thinking "parent" is just another word for money without end. This belief is prevalent in modern children, I've noticed.

"I need some money," says the penniless child to his parent.

"I don't have any," she replies, probably with some truth.

But the child has never lived who could be convinced his parent's wallet does not conceal a money machine, eternally grinding out cash on request. The child also is convinced the only reason he isn't getting his share of this unending money is that his folks just don't like him, or they are too selfish to share.

Thinking rich but talking poor has kept more adults out of the poor house than rich uncles have. This is especially true when children reach adulthood still convinced that mother is spelled M--O--N--E--Y.

All of this reminds me of several scenes from the childhood of my own children.

There was Steve, at age 5, watching a TV thriller about a woman who had hired a killer to bump off her husband. She wanted to collect his million-dollar insurance policy and share it with her boyfriend.

"When daddy dies, will you split the million dollars with us?" he asked, removing his thumb from his mouth and peering around his blanket.

Barb, age 4, dickered for a tricycle with her father, who was also brought up to speak "Poor" in the presence of his children. She peered into the empty billfold he showed her and asked, "Well, you can go to that place where you hide all the money and get some," she pointed out. A reasonable suggestion, I thought, in view of the fact she'd heard him mentioning going to the credit union to draw money out to pay for a new washer.

Holly, at 6: "You do too have money. Big people *always* have money. They just don't want to give it to little people."

Maybe not. But you can bet your bottom dollar (literally) little people will wage an all-out war to get the money away from the big people. Also, in some cases, they continue to wage their campaign long after they have become big people, capable of generating a money supply of their own.

One thing about a recession; money really is in short supply and it gets easier and easier for parents to say, in all honesty, that they don't have any -- at least not any that can be spent foolishly.

Laid off? Pink-slipped? The cold breath of inflation is frosting up your budget?

Think positive. For once in your life you can face your children and admit to poverty without guilt. Being able to tell the kids you're broke and not lie about it has its happy aspects. Besides, it's good for their character.

Slurp, gulp: the phantom eater struck again

For years we've had a phantom eater around our house and I know what you're thinking and you are wrong. It is not me. Phantoms are invisible, and when I eat I'm visible because people are always saying things like, "My gosh, not another second helping. Where do you get your big appetite?"

I began developing the phantom eater theory the other night when Joe emerged from the pantry with and empty Pop Tart box in his hand.

"Who at my Pop Tarts?" he demanded.

"Not me," Said his sister.

"Not me," Said his other sister.

"Not me either," said his other, other sister.

"Don't look at me," I said. "I hate Pop Tarts. Now if it had been your Ruffles with ridges or your French onion dip, you'd have cause to be suspicious. But Pop Tarts aren't my junky food habit."

In any event, the Pop Tart box was empty and no one in the family had touched them. Clearly, it was the work of the phantom eater.

The situation reminded me of the days when Joe's older brother lived home. Every afternoon he'd buy a bottle of Squirt on his way home from school to drink after he returned home from his job at the library.

"Don't anybody touch my bottle of Squirt," he'd warn, sticking the bottle in the back of the fridge. Somebody wasn't heading his warning because each night he'd return from the library to find the bottle, still in the same place, only empty.

"Who drank my Squirt?" he asked each night. There had to be a phantom Squirt drinker in the house because at the time there were 12 of us in our household and none of them would admit to touching his Squirt.

It was then I realized that there had to be a phantom addicted to Squirt who crept into the kitchen, while we were watching Howdy Doody and Kukla, Fran and Ollie, and finished off the Squirt.

Years passed and we noticed that the phantom ate up a lot of other goodies beside. We knew it was a phantom because no one else had eaten them.

Who at all the chocolate cookies?

Not me.

Who finished the coke?

No me.

Tell me who pigged down all the dip and I'll bust his face.

Not me, not me, not me.

One thing for sure, our phantom was not only a big sneak, he was addicted to junk food. You never heard anyone say who ate all the carrots? Or, who's the nerd who polished off the oatmeal?

Often when the phantom isn't gobbling down all of our goodies, it's in the bathroom using up the shampoo and the eye makeup and dulling the razor blades.

"Who used up the shampoo?"

"How should I know?" chorused the family. Have you ever heard our family chorus chorusing that great old tune, "How should I know?" You should sometime. They rank with the Trapp Family choir singing the Alleluia Chorus.

And how should I know but what they're not all singing the truth? All I know is that somebody keeps sneaking the Coke and Fritos and the chocolate chip cookies. And it sure isn't me.

Her nest runneth over

"Isn't it lonely with all of the kids gone?" I asked my neighbor as we sat in her immaculate, quiet kitchen, dawdling over a late Saturday morning cup of coffee. Undisturbed by anything save the soft strains of music from the stereo in the front room, she replied serenely.

"Oh yes, the kids, the ones who got married and left home this year. You know they'd completely slipped my mind this morning. I should give them a call and let them know that we're leaving for Florida next week."

Meanwhile, back at the kiddy ranch: Both bathrooms were full of girls washing their hair. Two television sets, one in the basement and one upstairs, entertained the neighbor youngsters with assorted Saturday cartoons. In separate bedrooms one child practiced her flute and the other his cornet.

There were dishes in the sink, the remains of last night's pizza party still in the living room. And on the stove simmered a post roast worth half a week's pay. In the laundry room the washing machine faithfully ground away at a weekend's supply of jeans and sweatshirts. A typical Saturday morning in what is supposed to be my empty nest.

For years I read all of those articles about something called the Empty Nest Syndrome. What they said was that when I reached middle age, all of my children would leave home and I would go insane.

My insanity, said the authors of these articles, would be caused by my grief at finding the house clean all day, being able to go away without paying a babysitter and finding ourselves financially solvent for the first time since our honeymoon.

They really believe this, these authors, they really do. Who do they talk to? Certainly not anyone with a real empty nest, or even anyone with a full one.

Anyway, here I am, middle age, ready to go insane because my nest is empty and I am no longer needed. So what do I find looking around? My empty nest is full of people. Two adults and three teenagers, not to mention Himself and I, and nobody shows the slightest inclination to leave home.

Meantime, if my peers, now lolling around in their empty nest, counting their money, and not listening to the Pink Panther on Saturday mornings, are finding this empty life difficult, they show no signs of it. Look at them over there, getting ready to vacation in Bermuda or running up north for a quiet weekend for two.

We have it figured out by the time our nest is empty, we should be in our nineties and then we'll have all kinds of time for such fun things as looking out the window or quick wheelchair trips to the dining room table.

For now we have a pretty fair schedule worked out. On Sunday morning, Monday, Tuesday, Wednesday, Thursday, Friday and Saturday morning THEY get to use the television, the phone, and the bathroom. Sunday afternoons and Saturday nights when THEY are away we get them. The empty nest syndrome means never having to wait your turn for the bathroom.

Blissful Quiet Descends upon Empty Nest like A Heavenly Mist

Some time ago I read a whole section in a magazine called, "The Problem of the Empty Nest." It told how mothers raise their families and after 17 years of the 22-hour day suddenly find themselves with the children almost raised and time on their hands. With a straight face it was asserted that many women get crazy from this sudden onslaught of peace and quiet.

Things like this are written usually by staff writers who have worked for years, live in New York and wouldn't recognize an empty nest if one dropped from a tree on their heads. "I'll bet you don't know what to do with yourself now that the children are all in school," say my companions in housework who must still chase preschoolers. In a pig's eye.

The first day I found myself entirely alone I toyed with the idea of running naked through the house singing and tossing rose petals about. However it was a chilly day and there was a chance that some other mother with an empty nest might drop in for coffee and I'd have to explain.

I told myself, this glorious euphoria at being alone would subside and I'd end up bored stiff. That was two years ago. The blissful quiet which follows the family exit still settles like a heavenly mist every weekday morning. And being able to enjoy a telephone visit without three interruptions every minute…well you can't imagine, unless your nest is empty.

Another heady pleasure is being able to leave the house without starting a riot in the nursery. The first year I was alone I walked to the store everyday savoring the fact that behind me were not a hundred wee voices screaming, " Mama, Mama, bring me a popsicle, a bubble gum, a candy bar, potato chips, a pop, a new bike!"

It's fun to go away at last without a diaper bag at my elbow and a play pen in the trunk of the car. The only hitch is, I must be home by 3:15 p.m., Cinderella, or the car will change into a pumpkin, and my name will be MUD if the children are locked out. But who can knock six hours of freedom, five days a week, from September until June.

Imagine if you will, young mothers, opening a can of paint without having someone under three trying to drink it the minute you turn your back. Picture your middle-age counterpart enjoying her afternoon nap without having to get someone else to sleep first.

And please don't ask in that pitying tone what I do with myself now that I am alone all day. I manage, believe me. If anyone else has a problem because they are no longer overrun with kiddies let them suffer. Me…I'm delirious. Sing Ho for the empty nest. Sing Hi for the quiet day!

Betty, Eddie, Ralph & John,

Herb & Steve

Barb, Betty & Holly, Trish

Chapter 5: To Sleep, Perchance to Dream?

Nap your way to fame

Napping can make you great. You've heard how Thomas Edison and Winston Churchill could work hours on end doing great things simply because they were able to take naps whenever they wanted.

Now researchers are looking into what napping can do for the average person, and as a napper of many years standing – or rather, lying down – I'm eagerly awaiting their results.

Napping never made ME great. Before I went to work and the children were all small enough to take afternoon naps, I napped every time they did. And I never got up and invented the electric light bulb, nor got elected prime minister of England. I just got up and fixed dinner.

Also, I was, according to my mother-in-law, committing a grave sin against the code of housewives by the act of hitting the chenille every chance I got. No decent woman she'd ever heard of fell into bed every time the children fell asleep.

I suspected she might have felt better had I spent the time in amorous dalliance with the milkman (if we'd had one). At least I'd have been awake doing something. But sleep? In the afternoon? The time should have been better spent folding laundry.

Still, tests conducted by the Naval Health Research Center have shown that people who napped scored better on tests than people who were deprived of sleep all day. The news item, passed on to me by a friend who knows my fondness for napping, failed to say what the tests were.

Did they include leaping up from the bed, saying loudly, "Ohmigod, it's a quarter to four and I haven't done a thing all afternoon?" If this had been one of the tests I'd have gotten 99 out of a possible 100.

Was one of the tests to see if you could vacuum a 10 room house, finish the laundry and get dinner ready in 40 minutes? And was there added handicap of a baby who needed a complete change and another who wanted to be dressed to go outside?

In this test, yours truly would have ranked in a modest way with nappers Edison and Churchill. The only difference between us was that they did their thing; I did mine; only I worked faster.

My children never inherited my fondness for taking naps, indeed they regarded an hour spent upstairs in their cribs as a criminal regards 30 days spent in "the hole" on bread and water. And they reacted accordingly.

For this reason I had to allow for them to fall asleep. During this time I was forced to stand guard to make sure they didn't break out of solitary (their cribs) and do things like drink nail polish or brush their teeth with mascara.

Naturally I didn't get much rest during the first hour, nor did I get much work done. But the following hour, "The Mother's Hour," I fondly liked to think of it as, I napped like a door mouse.

And it was at the magic moment of 3:45 that I was awoke each day and turned into Wonder Woman. Faster than a speeding bullet, more rapid than a locomotive, able to clean large rooms at a single bound.

Ah, those were the days. And this was why each day my husband would come in from work and say, "Gee, honey, you look all tired out. I'll bet those kids keep you hopping."

And I'd reply faintly, for by that time I really was faint, "You betcha!" Then it was time to count the hours until bedtime.

Just a lazy summer day

Anatomy of a summer afternoon nap:

1:00 p.m. - House is nice and quiet. Children have all left to play in the neighbor's yard. Perfect time for restful nap. Draw shade, shut bedroom door. Fall on the bed.

1:02 p.m. – Door opens. May Barbie and Holly go swimming? Certainly. Swim all afternoon. Where are the bathing suits? In Mother's closet? Spend 13 minutes searching. Suggest try own closet. Success. Close door. Fall back on bed.

1:15 p.m. – Door opens again. Where are nose plugs? Get up and look for nose plugs. Find them. Go back to bedroom. Shut door. Fall on bed.

1:20 p.m. – Door opens. Ice cream man is coming. May Joe have a Popsicle? Yes. Where is Mommy's purse? Ten minutes spent searching for Mommy's purse. Shut door. Fall on bed.

1:30 p.m. – Door opens. Ice cream man waiting. May Joe buy popsicles for all friends whose mothers were napping and couldn't give them money? No. No. NO. Fifteen minutes of angry debate. Ice cream man had become tired of waiting for customers and wandered away. Mother promises to buy Joe a Popsicle after nap if she is let along for 30 minutes. Agreed. Shut door. Fall on bed…at last.

1:45 p.m. – Knock on bedroom door. May John use the car for half hour? Sure, make it two hours. Pillow over head drowns out loud record player in living room. Patricia and friends are visiting and dancing.

1:50 p.m. – Door opens. Joe in tears. No one to play with. Friends all went to store to buy popsicles. Find dime for Joe. Suggest he walk very slowly to the store and back. Shut door. Fall on bed.

1:55 p.m. – Door opens. Patricia. Eye makeup is in mother's dresser drawer. Searches in all drawers. Asks for help. Eye makeup in bathroom. Sorry. Don't mention it. Not sleeping anyway. Shut door. Fall on bed.

2:00 p.m. – Door opens. Hinges showing definite signs of wearing out. Can we have a Kool-Aid sale? Yes, but not in mother's bedroom. Will mother get sugar down from top shelf? Also find pitchers? How about ice cubes? Make Kool-Aid. Return to bedroom. Shut door. Fall on bed. Reflect that falling on bed every two minutes great exercise. Really works a person out.

2:06 p.m. – Door opens. Kool-Aid spilled on kitchen floor. Much argument as to whose fault and who should mop up. Spend 30 minutes mopping kitchen floor. Girls home from swimming. Decide nap time is over. Wasn't sleepy anyway, just tired from so much falling on the bed.

2:10 p.m. – Too late for further napping. Too early to start dinner. House nice and quiet again. Children have all vanished and will not reappear again until time to eat. Pick up new magazine. Doctor in it says every mother should enjoy a quiet, restful nap each afternoon.

Best Rester on the Block

There is a poor housewife who doesn't have some small claim to fame for a task she does particularly well. There is the famous cook, the expert needlewoman, and the lady upon whom even Ann Landers could call before 9 in the morning.

There were others on my block well known for their polite children and white laundries. I was famous for my naps. Behind my back the other girls referred to me as Horizontal Betty. This was because anytime one of them came over I was stretched out on the couch, looking like the Lady of the Lake, only alive, sort of.

What I was actually doing was resting up between chores or any next encounter with the kids and my daily schedule looked something like this:

6:30 a.m. - arise, fix husband's breakfast and pack his lunch.

7:00 a.m. - lie down until time to wake the children.

7:15 a.m. - feed, dress, boot, mitten and coat the children, packing their lunches in between.

8:00 a.m. - lie down until strength returns, usually about 9:30 when the baby wakes for his morning feeding.

10:00 a.m. - rest again until 10:30 a.m.

10:30 a.m. - put the baby in his playpen; make some fresh coffee and call my girlfriend Elsie; wash dishes and fold diapers while visiting.

11:30 a.m. - take baby out of his playpen, change him and lie down until noon.

Later, of course, and the baby willing, I had my afternoon nap. It is easy to spot the woman who has raised her family and gone back to work. She's the girl who falls asleep at the typewriter every day between 1 and 2 p.m., the traditional nap time of every housewife and mother in the land.

I used to hear epic tales, from my in-laws, of course, about women who rose at dawn and never even went near a chair, let alone lie down, until late at night when everyone else was in bed. Naturally, our paths never crossed, they being too busy running around all day being epic and I busy resting.

Unfortunately, nobody ever came neighboring when I was standing up washing dishes or putting clothes in the washer. No, they always knocked on my door two minutes after I flopped down on the couch. So it was only natural that word of my horizontalness spread throughout the neighborhood.

One thing about women who always worked away from home; they seem never to have heard of people napping every day from 1 to 2 p.m., and tend to look upon their drowsy coworkers as suffering from some kind of pathetic handicap.

I never argued with my doctor when I was sick and he said to go home and get lots of rest. I just wondered what he thought I had been doing before I visited his office.

And I remember when my kindergartener came home and proudly told me the teacher had given him a star for being the "best rester in class," I smiled fondly. "It's a talent you inherited from your mother, child. Never forget that."

Nighthawk

There is probably a name for the condition. We just called it "that time the baby had his days and nights mixed up." I recall it as one of those periods which loomed unsurmountable in my life, like the ironing and the battle of unmatched socks.

From the minute he came home from the hospital, Nighthawk slept when we were awake and cried when we wanted to sleep. Surrounded by 40 or so screaming infants back in the hospital nursery, Nighthawk always seemed to be asleep.

"What a good baby," I'd say to anyone looking through the glass window with me, "I can hardly wait to get him home. He isn't going to be any more trouble than a stuffed panda."

Nighthawk was trouble. He had an unerring instinct for knowing when his careworn mother hit the sack, even in the daytime, or during one of his infrequent catnaps. The slightest creak of couch or bed was enough to bring him to screaming wakefulness.

Nighthawk was abetted by his older brother who never slept at all. He'd sneak into the room where Nighthawk's little crib was stashed and whisper evil plans into Nighthawk's sleeping ear.

"I'll get up at 6 so she can't sleep in," I think he said, "I can keep her busy all day long by spilling the diaper pail and climbing into the clothes dryer and by naptime she'll be exhausted and that's where you come in."

True, he was only 2 years old and didn't talk this way, but this is a translation from original baby pigeon. Nighthawk, asleep or awake, understood everything his brother ever said to him.

Big brother would lean into Nighthawk's bassinet, and later into his playpen, and murmur "anawana goggle glop ahwah." And Nighthawk would kick and smile and agree. You could tell he believed every syllable.

Meanwhile, back at the kitchen stove, Nighthawk's mother was beginning to look like the character of Charles Dickens who slept standing up. During Nighthawk's infancy I learned to peel potatoes and fold laundry while dozing.

"You should try and get out more," said Nighthawk's father, gently moving my head from my plate during dinner. That evening I got out to play bridge and won first prize without opening my eyes.

Night-times we took turns keeping Nighthawk Company. He'd take the 11 p.m. to 3 a.m. shift and then I'd fight the kid off until 7. By day I kept his bassinet in the kitchen where he could listen to the "top 40" and the noonday news and hear the other kids fighting.

It was no use, he was too exhausted by that time from his night of eating and crying and playing. Except for feeding, which he never missed and bath time which he slept through, he was good for the whole day and most of the evening.

Yes, we remember Nighthawk. How could we forget him? He's the one who doesn't wake up until his 10 o'clock tennis date. Only now he's asleep by 3 a.m. They do grow up.

Like Scotland Yard Motto – We Never Sleep

I used to know a woman who always said she was no good for anything all day if she didn't get eight hours sleep at night. She made quite a thing of it and it was quite distressing to be in a car with her at 1:30 a.m. stuck in an eight-foot snowdrift. It can and did happen if you are thinking, incredulous.

Anyway while the rest of the club was digging out the car so this particular member could get home and get her proper rest I began thinking back over my life.

Really, I think I was freezing to death. But suddenly I realized that I hadn't had a full night's sleep in 25 years. Maybe I haven't been good for much in the daytime over this period and this could be the reason.

We used to call our upstairs Scotland Yard, because its motto is, "We never sleep." And the children never slept. Oh I wouldn't say they never, never slept. From 9 until the 11 o'clock news things were pretty quiet. But they did seem to have a built in alarm system for when we were just drifting off to sleep.

If there was a baby on hand this was when he woke up for a bottle. Following him would be The One Who Went Potty at 12:45 every night. He was afraid of the dark and insisted that the place be lit up like a Polish cathedral before he would walk to the bathroom. The One Who Went Potty at 12:45 would fall asleep and then The One Who Had Bad Dreams got up.

He was never clear about what his bad dreams were, but made it very clear that he needed to be walked back to bed and tucked in again. The rest of the night we were kept busy with The One Who Wouldn't Be Weaned. He was the one I told you about before, and we were afraid that someday we might be packing his bottle along with his college things. He'd come stealing like a spirit in the night, balancing his bottle on his father's nose and snuffling loudly in his father's ear.

For what seemed like years we took turns getting up and going to the refrigerator to fill his bottle with cold milk. No one ever said a word during these pre-dawn interludes and The One Who Wouldn't Be Weaned glided silently back to his bed.

But they were all just babies then. Older heads assured us that as time passed things would settle down at night. Then the boys got in high school and the place really came to life after dark. They did homework, went out on dates or stayed up to watch the Saturday night late TV movie.

They slammed garage doors, entertained friends and wandered into the bedroom wondering where the pizzas were stored. Finally they left home and it looked like we might get some uninterrupted sleep.

And then the phone rang. It was our married son. "Sorry to bother you at two in the morning Mom. But can I come over and get my long underwear? I'm going hunting first thing in the morning."

Oh well, I couldn't have slept anyway.

Musical Beds every Friday

Saturday morning and one of THEM has just left with her pillow, her Monopoly game and her allergy pills. For years the children in this block have insisted the only way to show a chum they care is to invite them to stay overnight. So each Friday evening every kid on Brown Street under the age of 12 plays musical beds, and it takes their parents the rest of the weekend to sort them out again.

There Friday night friendship rituals are called Sleepovers, and during many years of sleepovers we have gotten to know every kind of child there is. Children who sleep over are Gigglers, Gabbers, Scamperers, Visiting Royalty, Compulsive Bathroom Goers and Cowardly Deserters.

The first time we heard a Giggler we were terrified. Did you ever hear a child laugh uninterrupted for three hours? We lay in bed wondering how to tell the mother of an otherwise nice kid that she had a real problem there. Gabbers aren't as disturbing, unless you regard having to yell, "Shut up and go to sleep!" every 20 minutes all night long as disturbing.

You fall asleep and wake at 1 a.m. The Gabber is still gabbing. At four, five and six you wake and she is still going. Your child has been asleep for hours, but this bothers the Gabber not. She came here to talk and by golly this is what she aims to do.

The Scamperers run around all night like a berserk squirrel. Run, run, run...the length of the hall and return. Around in circles. Up to the ceiling and back down the wall. "Boots, boots, boots, boots, moving up and down again. And there's no discharge in war." Next the Scamperer tells you what a nice rest she had all night.

Visiting Royalty is the only child of an older mother who only disapproves of such democracy. V.R. brings her own bedding, soap and monogrammed towels. With obvious difficulty her mother refrains from asking to inspect the sleep quarters for bugs and leaves written instructions about her child's breakfast menu and bedtime routine. Later she calls every hour to be assured that her darling is okay.

I once asked the mother of Compulsive Bathroom Goer if she didn't worry that her child got up every 15 minutes all night, and she said I must have her confused with another kid. "She's never done that I her life," said her mother. Well she does when she sleeps at our house, and furthermore leaves every light in the house burning when she goes back to bed. A Compulsive Bathroom Goer and a Scamperer make for a live house if they stay over on the same night.

The last of the darling visitors is the Cowardly Deserter who chickens out at 1:30 a.m. particularly if there is a blizzard or severe electrical storm going on outside. In 22 years I have escorted more Cowardly Deserters home through nights not fit for man no beast than any other woman in town. That oddball dashing past your house at 2 a.m. in bathrobe and slippers is not Wee Willie Winkie, girls, it's me. I guess I'm just another of those poor martyred mothers who has never learned to say no.

Hansen House on Brown Street, Saginaw MI

Chapter 6: Wheels

When kids get wheels

About the time parents are relieved of the 24-hour-a-day agony of wondering if their young are going to do themselves in by falling out of trees, running in the street, or hitting each other over the head with softball bats, another life shortener appears on the scene. The kids learn to drive.

Sure we have the mandatory driver education and other supposed safeguards. We also have kids drag racing on the side streets at midnight, if the even wait that late, and parents who for some unexpected reason buy new young drivers their own cars.

I will never forget the first automobile accident in our family. Actually it was the first for anybody, for a couple of generations, so you can imagine the reaction. The phone rang, Himself answered.

"Dad, I've got some bad news," said the young voice on the other end."

"You wrecked the car," declared father, with an astounding how of ESP.

"Not really wrecked it. Just messed up the front fender and wheel a little."

Like a good father, he asked the question a good father should ask.

"The car isn't important son, what is important is, are you alright?"

"Sure, I'm OK. Just a little shaken up is all."

"Good. I'm relieved to hear that because, my son, now that I know you aren't hurt, when you get home, I'm going to kill you." And so went the conversation for the rest of the evening and on and on and on the next day.

Such things are not taken lightly at our house. With a few teen-age drivers in the family, insurance rates being what they are, we regard a bashed-in fender a catastrophe comparable to an earthquake. Maybe this is why we've had so few of either.

In a more serious vein, neither will I forget the night one of our sons was injured in a much more serious auto accident. A friend picked him up and they hadn't been gone more than half an hour when we got a call.

"We have your son here at the hospital…no he isn't badly hurt…could you come right over?"

Suppose they are lying to us so we don't fall apart on the way over, we said to each other. It turned out they weren't lying, than heaven. But we will remember that drive to the hospital to the end of our days, and I think of it each time someone leaves with the keys to the family car.

Now we have a 15-year-old with a driver's permit (with mom or dad only is the stipulation). "But some of the other kids' folks let them drive alone anyway," she says.

"Well, you aren't going to be one of them," we insist. Nor will she have unlimited use of the car when that precious driver's license comes this fall.

If she wants a car she will have to wait until she is working and can afford one of her own. Many think we are a couple of mean, over-anxious parents. Maybe we are. But we will never forget that drive to the hospital, nor how lucky we were…that time.

License crisis arises again

Now there are six. Three of them are married and a fourth has his own car, so this leaves but two of the half dozen young drivers we have, in a manner of speaking, launched.

And I will say it again, as I have said before, "But dear, she's much too small and young to be old enough to drive an automobile. Maybe there's a mistake on her birth certificate or something. She doesn't look a day over 11."

"She's 16 years old," said her father. "I remember the night she was born, even if you forgot."

"But she isn't even big enough to see over the top of the steering wheel."

"Neither was you Aunt Mabel and she drove a car for 40 years."

What is there about the first driver's license? Why is it that I who cheered when they went off to kindergarten, felt no wrench when they graduated from high school and heave a sigh of relief the day they got married, go all to pieces when they tell me they are old enough to drive a car.

Having lived through this crisis five times before, I can tell you this. It seems as if one day you are taking the training wheels off their bikes and the next you are taking them for their driver's licenses.

I didn't really think that the boys were too small when they became licensed drivers, now that I remember. When the day arrived they were usually about six feet tall and what I said then was: "Well maybe he LOOKS old enough to drive, but he's just big for his age. Actually he's a six-foot 12-year-old."

And I hate to bring this up and sound cross and materialistic, but there's the matter of my car. I know that a parent is supposed to say, "I don't care if the car is totaled as long as my kid is OK."

This is ridiculous. In the first place it is impossible to bring a car home without a scratch unless the driver comes back in the same condition. This is, of course, providing that he or she didn't leave the car and stick his nose into someone else's trouble.

In the second place, I think most people are almost as worried about their cars as about their kids, only they don't think it sounds good to say so. So if you don't mind, when my daughter takes my car out for the first time without me, I am going to worry about it a teensy little bit.

And I will also worry about gas, having learned that a kid who drives can use as much gas going a mile to pick up a friend as his parents do driving to the Upper Peninsula. And in this age of shortages this is a lot to worry about.

Day of Freedom is just one driving test away

Little One, now soon-to-be 16, and now known as The Youngest Kid, received his driver's permit last month, to the joy of everyone involved except his older sisters.

I don't know why sending the youngest child off to school is supposed to be the high spot of a mother's life. It's said to mark the moment when she can finally be "fulfilled." Fulfillment, as defined by women's magazines, of course, means she can now leave home in the daytime without paying a babysitter.

Not so. A mother's real day of freedom comes when there is no longer anyone in the house who needs to be taken someplace by a parent. It reminds me of a plaque I say once on my summer travels which read, "If mother's place is in the home, then why am I always in the car?"

Anyway, back to Youngest Kid and his soon-to-be full-fledged driver's license. In today's world the driver's license is a Rite of Passage exceeded only by graduation and the wedding night, the latter being open to some question lately.

How well I remember when Youngest Kid's oldest brother took the family car for the first time. His father paced the floor, said his rosary and recited a litany of horrible eventualities, none of which came to pass, thank heaven.

When the second son became old enough to drive he'd calmed down a bit realizing that yes, indeed, kids do grow up fast. Then our daughters, one by one, followed in their brothers' footsteps, or in this case their drivers' seats.

"How can she be old enough to drive," asked Himself, "I just took the training wheels off her bike."

That was 10 years ago, I reminded him. She was indeed old enough to drive. And for a moment I envied parents of only children who get this thing over with all at once and get about the business of being "fulfilled" before they are aged or on the way to the funny farm, both of which I suspect is our current condition.

So now it's the turn of Little One, Youngest Kid almost grown up. Once again we are discovering how many trips to the store it really takes to buy a 12-pack of Coke: Would you believe one for each bottle?

We're becoming accustomed to the idea that nay venture involving the use of the automobile must also involve our son who "needs the practice." I know who is waiting for me with an errand the moment I pull into the drive. How well I know, having lived these moments many times before.

But soon it will be driver's license time for real, and once again pop will come in 12-pack containers, once again the car will resume its necessary status in our lives. And then we'll learn to live with the equation: automobile divided by five equals big family fight.

Meanwhile I feel like the mother of A.A. Milne's James James Morrison Morrison Weatherby George Dupree who said to his mother said he,

"You must never go down to the end of the town, if you don't go down with me." I suspect James James had just gotten his driver's permit and needed all the practice he could get.

Great White Whale – terror of Dixie Highway

Much as I hate the monster, I must admit, reluctantly mind you, that the Great White Whale, which is the name we've given our '68-vintage second car, is an excellent ad for elderly Oldsmobiles.

As a provider of transportation for my teen-age youngsters, who'd clearly prefer an MG, its adequate; the kind of car of which one can say, "It gets us there and gets us back. But it's not much."

Only in the case of the Great White Whale, it IS much; in fact it may be the largest old car in Bridgeport. But it does get them there and get them back, something of a miracle, in view of what it has to put up with.

The Whale, once a proud status symbol, is now the terror of Dixie Highway as it lumbers majestically along, undisputed king of the road.

"It's coming, get off the road, get the kids in the house, pull those VWs and Pintos into the garage…make way…make way."

At least this is what my children tell me the neighbors say. The neighbors are reluctant to discuss the White Whale with me for fear I'll really turn it loose on them. Actually, it's a gentle giant, even if it does take up the whole road.

In drive, the Whale is more docile than its reputation. It's when it is in reverse that it displays a lethal hostility toward anything behind it. The Whale is capable of demolishing whatever it backs into, fenders, fence posts, trees and objects we can no longer describe. And it moves regularly unscathed from these encounters.

We're sure that if we ever scrape off the coats of white paint, we'll find that the Whale is in reality a Sherman tank which has been hiding undercover since the Battle of the Bulge.

Like many of the elderly, the Whale has developed a few ailments here and there; here in Saginaw, a dead battery, there in Frankenmuth, a worn out heater hose. As a pet, it's almost as expensive as a cat or a youngster with braces on his teeth.

Where once I visited the obstetrician and pediatrician regularly, I now drop by our friendly little old village mechanic with a frequency that makes his week and breaks mine.

He doesn't look on the Whale as an automobile as much as he views it as a monthly income. This view is enhanced by the youngsters' talent for blowing out rusty old mufflers and backing into immovable objects.

The thing young drivers like least about it, aside from its advanced age, is that it's just not a "cool" car. And the Whale knows how they feel and retaliates by stalling on them at intersections and developing worn out parts when they take home crowds of friends they want to look "cool" to.

The Whale, says my friend the mechanic, who doesn't want me to sell it and lose half his weekly income, is safer than a compact car. "The children are much safer in it than they'd be in one of those little jobbies," he says wisely.

True, I agree, writing out another check for repair of the Great White Whale. But one of these days, things must change. Either by the end of 1977 we'll have replaced so much of the Whale that it will be a brand new car, or we'll have a different car. The Whale will be in Oldsmobile Heaven, and the world will once again be safe for fence posts, trees and other immovable objects we're unable to describe anymore.

The village Volkswagens will no longer have to stay off the streets when the Whale is at large, but my friendly neighborhood mechanic may be out of business. It's tough deciding what to do with an aging whale.

Chapter 7: Fatherhood

Solver of problems, fixer of the unfixable

The very first thing I can ever remember about my father was sitting on his lap and learning to read from newspaper headlines when I was 4. Thanks to him I became the only 4-year-old on the block able to read phrases like "Chicago slaying," and "Gangland war," and "Stock market crash." My early education was nothing if not contemporary.

The first things I can remember thinking about my father were that (1) he owned the telephone company, and (2), he was an engineer on a railroad train and also Indian. I was a good reader but otherwise a little dumb.

I wasn't too disappointed to learn he didn't own the telephone company, only worked there. I was a bit let down to find that the kind of engineer he was didn't run trains. The only way he really let me down was by not being Indian.

The kids who lived in the various neighborhoods where we moved when I was little always said, "Oh, your name is Morningstar, you must be Indian." And I'd go home and ask, "Daddy, are we Indian?" And in his funniest joke of the century he'd just reply, "Ugh!" I never knew what my mother thought was so funny.

Well, of course, once I found out we weren't Indian I was obliged to say something like, "No, we're German with a name that was translated." But nobody ever said you had to meet an obligation. I lied about it for a long time. To this day some people still think I'm Indian. What do I care? I like Indians.

Dad spent a good share of his time traveling around Michigan supervising the "cutover" from the old operator-manned telephone boards to the automatic dial systems. For years were referred to him as "Daddy-is-out-of-town."

But his homecomings were joyful occasions and he never forgot to bring us something, a toy or a small treat, buried in his suitcase. To this day I never smell leather luggage without thinking of my father. I had to get to be a parent and traveling around a bit myself to know that it took trouble to stop into a store and buy toys on a business trip.

Even if he wasn't an Indian railroad engineer who owned the telephone company, we grew up believing our father was smart and respected by everyone in town, except on occasion, by his mouthy offspring.

From the day my mother first told the story of how, as a young telephone linesman, he'd climbed a telephone pole and plugged in his test set to call the doctor the night I was born, I believed my father could do anything.

He of the bottomless wallet, the solver of problems, the fixer of the unfixable had -- and still has -- and unwavering optimism about life, a gift he shared with me.

Figuring out the family finances for a Depression-hit family of seven, he would look up from a scrambled budget and say happily, "Another few months and we'll be out of the woods." Financially he never got out of the woods until his family grew up and left home, but in all those years he never lost hope.

On my wedding day, waiting to escort me up the aisle, he offered to cover for me if I wanted to make a fast retreat. In later years when I went home to mother, both times he lectured me and sent me back.

The last time I saw my father was in April in St. Petersburg, although we visit almost weekly on the phone. Still serene, hopeful, in charge and busy with life and full of opinions.

And when I read so much about children with absent fathers and the lack of a male image in a home or a poor one at best, I am saddened. Good memories of your father are nice things to have on Father's Day.

Such little things remind me of my dad

We were talking about our fathers, my friend and I. Stories from our childhood, our first perceptions of these most important men in our lives – men who were the foundation for how we would forever perceive the opposite sex.

Such delicate scraps of memory they were.

"My father was a working man," she said. "I remember once he took me on a train trip. I fell asleep and after a while I awoke to hear him talking to the man in the next seat. They were discussing world affairs and the stock market.

"All of a sudden I realized my father was a very intelligent man. I had always been a little ashamed of the fact that he worked in a factory. But who knows the circumstances which locked him into that life."

And then she said, "Sometimes such little things remind me of my dad."

A sight, a sound, a smell — and a fragment of time drifts by: The sight of a tall stooped man carrying a battered lunch pail; the smell of machine oil, her husband's clothes after he's been working on his car; the relentless humming sound of an industrial plant heard across the river on a hot summer night.

She remembered her father on payday. He always brought her a present when he cashed his check, a nickel tablet with a picture of an Indian on the cover. She would scribble "stories" in it by the hour then take them to her mother and ask, "What did I write?"

And her mother would fill the scribbled pages with fantasy spun from her own busy brain as she prepared the evening meal.

Each night his lunch pail contained something special for her, usually a cupcake or cookie her mother packed for his dessert.

"I suppose my mother packed two, one for him and one for me. But it didn't matter. If there had only been one, he would still have brought it home to me and done without.

Such tiny fragments of our lives they are, these things forgotten, until one day a sight or sound or smell brushes the senses, spinning the mind backward through time and I am reminded of my own father as a young man.

The sound of a car turning into the drive next door; a man's voice greeting his children at their back door; the smell of newly-raked leaves in October twilight; the sound of workers swarming out of a tall office building, homeward bound on a snowy winter night.

"Do kids still wait for their father to come home from work each night?" I asked my friend. "That used to be the high spot of our day. And I remember when he went out of town on business, he always brought presents back for us – a book of cutouts for me and maybe a toy car for my brother. I remember thinking, 'My father must be very rich and important.'

"I remember his hopefulness – sitting at the dining room table with my mother, going over the bills, saying happily, 'Well, we'll soon be out of the woods.' They never did get out of the woods financially until we kids were grown up and away from home."

An old man in the drugstore, waiting for his prescription to be filled, making small talk with the pharmacist; the sound of old men's voices coming through an open window on a sunny afternoon; the smell of cigar smoke on an old man's dark blue sweater.

Such fragile scraps of time they are, these memories we somehow lose. But once in a while one of them drifts past the window of the mind like a golden autumn leaf and, for a little while, we catch and hold that time again.

There's a man in our house!

"He yells at us sometimes. But if we look at him with sad faces we know he won't spank us. He doesn't like to hit anyone," say his children.

"He knows how to balance checkbooks," says his wife, "checkbooks with un-numbered checks and checkbooks with no amounts written down. No one in the family can figure out how he does this. He is a magician with figures." Nor does his family know how he always manages to scrape up the money for college tuitions, doctor bills, clothes, Christmas and birthday presents. They think he's a financial wizard, also a millionaire.

Sometimes he must be off to work before his family is awake. But he doesn't forget if it is a special day. Once his daughter found a surprise greeting on her 13th birthday – a supermarket sack propped up on the kitchen table. "Happy Birthday to my darling teen-age daughter," it was in bright red crayon. She still has it. Another morning when the family was all down with the flu, he left an orange for each one inked with an individual get-well message.

He's never too busy to listen to his wife when she's had it up to her eyelashes with practically everything. He never says, "Don't tell me your troubles. I've got enough of my own." No, he waits until she had finished spouting off and then says, "Honey I don't blame you a bit. If I were in your shoes I'd feel exactly the same way." Then his wife feels a lot better and quits complaining. This is very nice, and besides if she feels really miserable he takes her out for dinner to help her forget whatever it was she was mad about.

He could be the best repairman in the world, having rebuilt toasters, washers, dryers, bicycles, irons and many other items far beyond the "planned obsolescence" manufacturers were supposed to have in mind for their goods. He can fix automobiles and knows how to hang pictures without knocking three feet of plaster from the wall. His family considers this a great stunt.

He worries a lot. His wife and children keep telling him not to worry about them, that they'll be okay. But he keeps right on. He worries when any of them are away for the evening, imagining accidents and other catastrophes. He worries about whether he will be able to send all of his many children to college and sometimes he worries about their future and the kind of world they face.

He is so proud of his family and says his wife and daughters are beautiful, and his sons the handsomest, smartest boys who ever lived. His family is not always too sure he is right in this, but it is wonderful to know somebody thinks that way. And often when the time is right and they need to know it most, he will tell them how much he loves them. He is a wage earner, a husband and a father. He is the man in our house. Happy Father's Day, Dear.

Herb and Betty

Chapter 8: Housekeeping

Homemaker was happy, most of the time

Was I ever a happy homemaker? Was there a time when I looked with joy and satisfaction upon a house I'd cleaned myself, when a trip to the PTA was a big night out?

These are questions I asked myself as I wrote this week's story on happy housewives. With some reservations, the answer is "Of course." Do you think I could have written about the job for 10 years straight without running out of funny stories if I hadn't enjoyed myself?

So I made domestic history by never cleaning the kitchen stove and finally throwing it out and getting a new one. That doesn't mean I wasn't having a good time while the stove went un-cleaned.

Sure I was the one who sewed myself to the slipcovers I was making, locked the meter man in the basement and went away and forgot he was down there and kept a pet field mouse in an old aquarium in the kitchen.

This doesn't mean I felt hampered by my role in life and all that stuff. You might think it means I was in the wrong job. At the time I didn't think I was. Would you believe me if I told you I was happy in the center of this uproar?

While the stove went un-cleaned, I painted (and repainted) every single room of an 11 room house and refinished the paneling and much of the old furniture we'd inherited from folks who could afford better stuff.

I breast-fed infants, was lulled by the soft, dove-like sounds they made, and delighted in the feel of their small bodies against mine. And while dishes say in the sink, I read to children or made them homemade play dough and fingerprints out of starch.

Basting my pants to a slipcover ruffle I held on my lap as I sewed made a funny story to tell the family and later the world. The slipcovers themselves were beautiful and my heart sang with happiness each time I walked into the living room.

No, I can't say I ever felt frustrated or deprived of a chance to use the talent God gave me. I wrote and sold what I wrote. The typewriter stayed on a table in my kitchen so I could work with my dinner cooking and the little ones in a playpen at my side.

I had a man who loved me, who took delight in the things I did and said and who told me I'd be rich and famous someday. I never quite made it, but it was nice knowing someone thought I might.

There were people in my life who sustained me through the bad times and gave me a lift with the work when I needed it, which was often. And there was, with me anyway, a certain sense of freedom.

Freedom to create, to do a good work, take a walk with the children on an autumn day or visit with a friend: these were the fringe benefits of a job I left behind me when the time was right, and long before I learned it was the one which drove other women to drink and pills.

I found I had much in common with the happy housewives I interviewed. One attitude we shared, although our lifestyles varied greatly. This is an appreciation of the day at hand, the hour and the moment.

As I write this, I have a feeling it is probably more acceptable to share with people all of the rotten times of your life so they can feel sorry for you. To come right out and say that you've been blessed with a wonderful life could be interpreted by some as boasting.

I hope not. Rather, I hope it is a sharing with others of the secret that each day is a gift to be used well, to be enjoyed. And I am also sure that the women I talked with will enter each phase of their lives with the same happy approach they have now.

Magnolia: the bloom lingers

I had never hired a cleaning woman before and hoped, humbly, that I was worthy of one. Rummaging through the storehouse of my mind a few nights ago, I stumbled across a memory of her voice the first time we ever talked. "Honey," she said sympathetically, "I'll be there as soon as I can work you in amongst my rich folks."

She knew I wasn't rich, probably sensed over the phone that her wages were coming out of my grocery money. But she didn't care and heaven knows, with an 11-room house and all of those children, I needed a little help.

I don't know why I never told you about Magnolia before. Maybe it's because, for some years now, it hasn't been fashionable to write about a black woman unless they were doing something with more of a future than day work.

Magnolia made a career of housework until age forced her into semiretirement. I used to wonder how she could go forth daily to work so hard without dropping in her tracks. She told me she was used to it. But sometimes I'd scrub my house from top to bottom to see what it was like to be Magnolia and I was never sure.

Magnolia was another of those strong, energetic older women who, with their childbearing years behind them, came into my life to give a hand with the housework and babies and listen in sympathy to this dream I had. The dream that one day all this would be behind me and I could write books or be a reporter for a newspaper. I was luckier than many women.

Magnolia's day at my house was the high spot of the week. I suspect it wasn't the high spot of hers; coming as she did from beautiful homes where wealthy people didn't stay home long enough to get anything dirty.

No place else did she find a roll of toilet paper on the dining room table. No place else did she work around four children under the age of 7. I was endlessly surprised that she showed up for work at all.

She left my house smelling of lemon polish, and pine-scented cleaning powders and floor wax. For a day or two, until the children caught up with the place again, we gleamed and sparkled like a television soap opera house. I used to promise myself that when I grew rich, I'd have Magnolia come every day in the week.

The best part of our day was lunch when, the babies in for their naps, we could settle down to share sandwiches, coffee and our lives. Her conversation was a treasure trove of tales of her "rich folks," and she had a way of calling my attention to the life I was missing when I couldn't see the outside world through the kids.

Magnolia was the only cleaning woman I ever had, mostly because she was the only one who understood why I was such a complete washout on the domestic scene. Magnolia agreed that, for me, the typewriter took precedence over the dusting. I never had to be one of those women who clean the house before the cleaning lady comes.

After a while, I really couldn't afford to pay someone to clean my house and besides, I told myself, the three girls were getting older and they should equal one Magnolia.

Magnolia moved on to other, probably easier work assignments, the children were all in school and I went to work myself.

Once in a while she calls me up, and we talk about when the kids were little and about the old house and the way things were when she was one of the best happenings in my house-bound existence.

She's always talking about getting together for lunch one of these days, but somehow it never works out. I wish it would someday.

Mom learns labor laws: Kids + Work = Confusion

Something tells me that Walter Reuther and The Big Three couldn't care less, but right now I am in the midst of negotiating a new labor-management contract with the children. It is now secret around the neighborhood that I have the largest payroll and pay the highest wages of any mother-employer on the block.

I'm an easy boss. The kids like the short working hours, the free pop and the stipulation that jobs completed when 'Dark Shadows' comes on at 3:30 p.m. It's a little hard on the slowpokes who rise at noon, but they understand after I yell a little.

What is really bogging down our contract talks is the business of job classifications and duties. Like last night when it was Patricia's turn to clear the table and Barbara's turn to load the dishwasher.

"Mo-th-er! You tell her. The dishwasher loader wipes the cupboards and sweeps the floor."

"But I can't reach the cupboard unless I stand on a chair. And she puts all the food there for me to put away, and that's the table cleaner's job."

"There isn't any place else to put it when you take it off the table. I think it should be the dishwasher loader's job." This dissention is by no means confined to KP duty. The one who cleans the two living rooms has to make our bed, but does not touch the bathroom. Whoever cleans the bathroom also does the TV room. Putting away folded laundry is preferable anytime to unloading the dishwasher and putting away the dishes, for no discernible reason.

It gets complicated sometimes. Just this evening I noticed that no one had pushed the button on the dishwasher. Angrily I threw open the back door and called to Barbara who was just getting on her bike. "Barbara Sue, you come right back in here and push the button on the dishwasher."

"I cleared the table tonight. That's the dishwasher loader's job. Call Patricia." She left quickly before I could argue.

My husband left Huntley and Brinkley long enough to visit the kitchen. "I hope you don't' mind me asking. I know you're very tired, but is it too much trouble for you to push the button on the dishwasher yourself?"

"That shows all you know about labor management relations," I said indignantly. "Do you realize that if I ever pushed the button myself, I'd lose face, respect, prestige and all of my authority with those children? The mother never pushes the button on the dishwasher. Hey, where are you going?"

"Out for a beer, to be alone and think for a while. I just can't make myself believe I've heard all of this."

Oh well, contract time is hard on everyone.

Souvenirs useless yet precious

September is a time for cleaning house they say. A time to air the winter clothes, tidy the bookshelves and bring in all the plants. And certainly it's time we got rid of all that junk laying around the shelves and tables collecting dust.

Here is a plaster model of a hand, enameled bright red, hanging on the wall. Joe made that last year in school and brought it home as a Christmas gift. On the shelf nearby is his egg carton caterpillar with yellow pipe cleaner antennae and a coat of bright pink tempera. Where in the world will I ever again find a pink caterpillar with purple sequin eyes? No, the caterpillar stays right where we placed it last spring.

How could I possibly throw out this napkin holder made of Popsicle sticks which Holly made last time she was in the hospital? True it is too fragile to hold napkins. But it took much patience and glue to put all those Popsicle sticks together into anything. The Popsicle holder stays.

And this plastic cake ornament, a miniature basketball player with the numeral 33 on its back. John doesn't want it anymore, but he says he doesn't want me to throw it away, and of course his trophy remains right next to somebody's collection of fresh water clam shells.

Whose "pretty stones" are these laying in a neat row on the bottom shelf? Somebody who'd be very hurt if I tossed them out, I'll bet. And I've completely forgotten who made the red painted coffee can decorated with Indian symbols, or the papier-mâché turkey.

Does anyone really want this stuffed baby alligator we brought back from Florida last fall? Probably. Is some member of the family emotionally attached to a tiny trophy which says, "To the Greatest?" If I had any idea as to the greatest "what" or "who," why then I might know whose prize it is.

A tiny cup from Niagara Falls…our son and his bride brought back form their honeymoon; a scarlet enamel tray sent from a friend when she visited San Francisco; an empty vase with the inscription, "Your 25th Anniversary!"…all useless, idle and priceless to someone.

This piñata sent clear from Mexico and doomed it seems to stay with us forever. Once, hopefully we sent it to school, delighted that for the first time in years we no longer had a dusty purple piñata in the corner of the dining room. But alas, our piñata came back alive, thanks to a teacher who thought it too pretty she carefully removed all of the goodies through a small hole in the back, closed it again and returned our souvenir.

Tenderly I replace a small bunch flowers remembering a frosty fall morning my husband brought them to me from the market. Our collection grows and how can we decide what we no longer need or want? How many souvenirs does it take to add up to a life time?

Thanks for the memory

Then night I left the house saying to my daughters, "Now when I return I want to see an immaculate kitchen." And when I returned to the same mess remained with much added to it. "We didn't know what immaculate meant," they wailed by way of excuse. "Did you try the dictionary?" "We couldn't. Your desk was so messy we couldn't find it."

There was the day the Bishop called up and our three-year old dashed to the phone, grabbed it and said his first bad word. I was afraid to apologize for fear the Bishop might not have understood my child and would ask, "For what?" And I could hardly ask if he's heard right, so I'll never know whether he did or not.

Another memorable time began the night before when an energetic cowboy-playing son leaped upon his mattress and stabbed it with his Cub Scout knife. "Well, this ends having a Christmas tree this year," said his father. (He's always hanging himself like that. "We'll have to use the tree money to fix the mattress."

But we did have a tree that year, a free one in fact. Because the mattress stabber told the principal he knew a very poor family in the neighborhood who wouldn't have a Christmas tree and she told him to give them the big one that stood in the school hall.

I remember well the day two of the boys found some paint and painted "Zorro the Great" all over the back of the house of a neighbor who hated all children anyway. And the night one of them broke out with chickenpox at the Longfellow School PTA meeting and started an epidemic.

History was made the day John stopped a train at the age of two and a half by standing on the tracks. If the train had not been the Beeliner it would have been John's last stand. It made us and the C&O Railroad very unhappy, and John's father made it painfully clear that we didn't think it was one bit cute.

Who could ever forget the day Ralph and a chum, whose dad was a policeman, locked Ralph into one side of a pair of handcuffs, while the folks were out of town, and then unexplainably locked the other cuff onto the milkman who came in and tried to be helpful? We never forgot and neither did the policeman or his wife or the milkman.

Nor could we forget the summer evening when Patricia was four and found the newsboy's sack in the grass and delivered all his papers all over the neighborhood while the boy was getting in a little extra baseball on his route. At least he never tried it on our block again.

When you have raised a family there are so many tender, endearing memories. And sometimes I ask myself, "Wouldn't you give anything to live those happy days over again?" And I quickly reply, "Good Lord, no!"

My supernatural powers

I know you are never going to believe this, but for years my family has been convinced I possess supernatural powers of a sort, in that it is I who makes things either appear or disappear around the house. "Hey, where are my short?" yells my husband from the bedroom.

"Where else, in the middle drawer."

"Oh no they aren't. I've been through that drawer twice. Somebody must have moved them."

My moment…I walk to the bedroom and fish his shorts from the middle drawer, where I put them yesterday, but where they apparently remained invisible until the proper person – me – appeared on the scene. This is the only conclusion we can offer. What do you think?

I don't like to brag, but I can also do this in reverse. Or so I am told. Like when he gets an ash tray out of the cupboard and puts it on the kitchen table and when he turns around from the refrigerator with his open can of beer the ash tray has vanished.

"Where'd my ash tray go?" he demands.

"How should I know?"

"You did something with it."

"I did not."

"Then how did it get into the sink with the dirty dishes?"

"Beats me."

"Hold this for me," says one of the children, handing me a shoe or a book. In two minutes, said object has not only vanished, but I can't remember where it vanished when the phone rang or the over buzzer sounded.

"It's gone for good," they gloom. "Mom had it in her hands for 30 seconds." Usually it isn't gone forever. Days later we find it on top of the refrigerator, or under the bed, which are odd places to shove things when the phone rings. But this is an odd house some days.

But I redeem myself at "hunting for galoshes" time. There has never been a more skillful, clever or more supernatural hunter-upper of boots, mittens and odd shoes in the world, the reason being that if I didn't conjure them up some way, somebody might stay home from school all day.

The tough part of being able to make objects come and go like this is nobody in the house even bothers to look for anything. Standard procedure is to call up the genie by standing in the middle of a room yelling, "I can't find my whatchamacallit any place."

And then the gentle genie, who doesn't really want to be called, suggests, "Its right where I put it, under the desk."

And they reply, "No it isn't. I looked there 10 times." But the genie, lying on the living room couch, reading the latest issue of Occult Quarterly knows it really is under the desk and she can make it appear. This is how we genies operate, you know.

Leaping Lizards its Trapper Tot

Have I ever told you about the time I met a four-inch crayfish crawling in my front hall? Or did you know about the morning I went for my second cup of coffee and noticed that a jar containing a bat was staring at me from the center of the table? The kids are born hunters and trappers, and if you were lost in the woods with them, you could stay alive, provided you could eat butterflies, caterpillars and fried mice.

The most terrifying words a mother can hear when her child, Trapper Tot is growing up is, "Mom, quick get me a jar with some holes poked in the top!" A word of advice: never, never respond to the cry of "Mom, quick get me a jar with some holes poked in the top!" Have you ever heard a Scot yell, "Mom, quick get me a tank for this Loch Ness Monster!?" Did anybody answer?

You're darn right they didn't. And you won't either if you know what's good for you. Anything that needs to be brought into the house in a jar with holes poked in the top shouldn't be brought in the house. How do you explain to a gigantic bumble bee who just escaped, faster than a hornet, from his ventilated jar that you had nothing to do with his capture? While he is chasing you around the house, how do you get him to stop trying to kill you, long enough for you to explain it's your 6-year-old son Trapper Tot he's after? What do you say to a bird your daughter thought was sick but isn't when it is having ten kinds of a fit about being in your kitchen? Will that pair of hornets in the baby food jar ever understand that you weren't out to get them before they got you?

Prior to my career as a mother, I enjoyed only a passing familiarity with the rest of the animal kingdom. Outside the zoo, I'd met an occasional dog and cat, being a city kid, had been told about cows and horses. It was not until Trapper Tot that I found out I could also eat lunch with a schoolboy who insisted his pet snake remain around his neck while he finished his vegetable soup. I have another rule about kids. If one of them comes to the door with his hands cupped around an unseen something and says "Let me in," I run to the door and lock it. Then I run to the other door and lock that too. And just to be sure, I check the screens. Never, never let a kid into your house who has something hidden in his hands.

If it was something you wanted in the house he wouldn't have to hide it. If it was dead, he wouldn't be holding it like that. He's being sneaky that's what. Whatever it is he's trying to bring into the house should probably be in a jar with holes poked in the top, and you don't' want that in here either. Another danger area for mothers are small boy's pockets. Here your dilemma is double. Do you reach into his pocket before your wash to embrace a handful of dead baby frogs? Or do you come down later to find they are all floating around in the washing machine?

How many angels can dance on the head of a pin, asked St. Augustine? How many dead baby frogs can be carried off in the spin cycle of your washing machine? How come these kinds of things never happen to Barbara Walters, and where did you ever pick up the idea that motherhood was an uplifting career? Anyway, I've always wondered what Jane said to Boy when he came climbing up the tree to their house and said, "Hey mom, quick, get me a jar with some holes poked in the top!"

The Great Organizer

The schedule on the kitchen bulletin board outlining the children's weekly tasks proclaims me as a well-organized, duper efficient Parent's Magazine type of mommy: the kind who writes those little squibs, helpful hints for mother's like: "I never have trouble organizing my housework even if I am the mother of 10 children under the age of 9. I merely assign each child his particular chores each week and spend all of the leisure time watching TV and reading confession magazines.

Where the whole system falls apart is when my own four children under the age 17 begin reading the assignment chart and reassigning the work I have laid out for them.

"That's my Girl Scout night, Barb can take the kitchen for me".

"I baby-sit right after school on Wednesday. I'll let Trisha take the living rooms then."

"Holly can do bedrooms and bathroom on Friday. I'm supposed to do some make-up work at school."

And then it's time to go to work.

Why isn't the kitchen done?" I ask crawling in from the office at 5 p.m. to face the breakfast dishes.

"It was Barb's day for the kitchen."

"That's what it says on the chart," Barb defends herself. "But she owes me two kitchens from last week and one living room from this week."

"Why does she owe you two kitchens?"

"Because she went shopping one day and baby-sat the other."

"When did you kids begin borrowing each other's chores?"

"Doesn't everybody?"

"I don't know. Does everybody?"

"I owe Holly one upstairs bedroom and one folding clothes."

"Where was Holly when all of this was going on?"

"She had to babysit."

"Well what about the schedule I put on the wall?"

"How can you make a schedule for us when you don't ask what we are supposed to be doing?"

"Ye gods, how can I ask you what you are doing when you're never home?"

And so it goes. Like the British Empire we somehow muddle through. Me with my efficient schedule tacked on the kitchen bulletin board; they with their own efficient method of chore borrowing and lending. But it doesn't leave me much time for leisure. I rarely watch TV or read confession magazines.

Soak Saga

What's wrong with washing pans and scouring dishes? Has our youth become so soft and flabby they are no longer capable of a little elbow grease in the doing of the dishes? For that matter, were they ever capable?

The thing that seems to happen around our house is that about once a month I get ready to cook a meal, and find there is nothing to cook it in or on. The broiler is dirty. All of the casseroles are stored in the refrigerator or freezer with a dab or two of leftover "Zesty Delight" drying out or turning green as the case may be.

Pans? The pans are soaking. The family dishwashing crew has a method for doing pans. If they can squeeze them in the refrigerator, contents and all, they do so. If, oh joy, they had nothing stuck or dried in them, they go into the dishwasher.

Otherwise they soak, and soak and soak. After a while there isn't even a clean space on the cupboard for making peanut butter sandwiches. It's covered solidly with soaking pans.

"Somebody had better get at those pans," we tell our dishwashing crew.

"Tomorrow is Holly's night for the dishes. I'll save them for her," is the reply. That's another thing about our dishwashing crew. Each night is initialed for whose night for the dishes. Yet, somehow, on the bad nights, the greasy pans, the horrible casseroles always fall on Holly's night. Naturally Holly is the youngest dishwasher and therefore least privileged.

"I'd show them," says their father, "when you get ready to fix a meal just tell them we can't eat because there is nothing to cook in and no serving dishes."

I do this and they should be crushed. They aren't. They are delighted. "Does that mean we can go to McDonalds for hamburgers and French fries?" they ask hopefully.

"No, it means that before I fix you a good wholesome family-type meal, you are going to have to wash all of the pans and bowls on the cupboard and in the refrigerator.

140

"It's Holly's night for the kitchen. Get her to do it."

"Whose night was it Thanksgiving?" my husband wants to know surveying the large water-filled turkey roaster.

"I can't remember," replies our oldest daughter, "that was three months ago."

"Well, somebody had better get busy on the pans. We've got to eat sooner or later."

"I've got it," suggest another child, "How about roasting wieners over the gas stove on the marshmallow forks?"

"No good," replies another. "They've been soaking since July."

Uppity worldly goods

Yes, now that you mention it, I do go all to pieces when I can't find anything, which could account for the shattered state I seem to be in most of the time. Some people always know where things are when they want them. I rarely know where anything is on the first try.

And we all know who is responsible for the fact that nothing is where I think it is, don't we?

Who has my blusher in her handbag, and is on the bus, halfway to school by now? Who put eyebrow tweezers and the small mirror under her bed? And who will deny it staunchly, as I am rushing around the house, screaming accusations to the four winds?

But who will apologize when the eyebrow tweezers and the small mirror are found when we change her bedroom around next spring? Nobody, that's who. The same nobody who says' she didn't put my blusher in her handbag, or forgot where she put the eyebrow tweezers.

"Why are you always accusing people of losing your things?" my husband asked, as he fished my handbag from under the living room sofa. "Who, but you, would sit in the living room, rummaging through your purse and then hide it under the sofa?"

"I'm sure I don't know," I said carrying all of the family hairbrushes down from the girl's bedroom. "But it certainly can't be me. I don't do things like that."

"Who has be wearing my rain coat?" I demanded, the other morning. "It has makeup all around the collar."

"Don't look at me," said Barbara. "I only wear a size 5 and that's about a 16. And besides, I don't wear makeup."

"And for Pete's sake, don't look at me," my husband said. "When was the last time you saw me in a pink paisley raincoat with gold buttons?"

OK. I'll concede that. But, on the other hand, who moves my paperback books when I am our in the kitchen making a snack or going to the bathroom? A paperback book, lying face down on a table, just doesn't sprout legs as soon as my back is turned, does it?

And it doesn't just move to another part of the house, either, but gets up and leaves town forever, without even so much as a farewell explanatory note.

Other people put a coffee cup down and momentarily misplace it. Who else's coffee cup vanishes into the air with nary a trace, never to be seen or heard of again?

I have the only winter shoes in town that fly south in the fall. If this isn't true, then how come they vanish in September, after sitting in the closet all summer, only to reappear, looking fresh and rested, in the spring?

And how about those clothes hangers that vanished last August. One day we found several hundred of them had moved to Lansing and were staying with John at college.

"If you had a place for everything and everything in its place, you wouldn't always have to be hunting," my mother-in-law used to say. She always like to make people feel good.

"Oh, I do, I do," I'd reply. "The real problem is that I know where everything should be. I just don't happen to own anything that knows its place. My life is full of uppity worldly goods.

Our little ups and downs

If it happens that we should have to gather a few precious belongings together and leave our home in a hurry, I know exactly where I will find everything we need or value.

First I'll go to the middle drawer in the kitchen which I've already told you about. If I can get it open, I'll take whatever is there. Next I'll sweep into a large supermarket sack all of the important stuff people have been shoving on the top shelf of the front hall closet all these years.

Then I will gather up whatever is on the table by the front stairs and also the things which are piled up on the chair next to the basement steps.

It has long been a family custom to deposit family laundry and other items, supposed to be upward bound, on the table by the front stairs. And it is also customary to leave anything going to the basement on the chair by the basement steps.

The thought behind this is that whoever is going either upstairs or downstairs can grab whatever is on the table or chair and take it up or down, depending, as a service to the rest of the family. That's the thought. It isn't a very intelligent one.

"On your way up (or down) take those towels (or hammer) will you?"

"OK."

"Grab that pile of jeans on your way up, will you?"

"OK."

"Would you mind taking those tools downstairs with you?"

"OK."

Those 'OKs' are strictly for sound effects to fill in vacant spots in our family communication. They mean nothing in the way of action, because for years we've been living out of those two piles, one by the basement door, and the other by the front stairway. The rest the family's important stuff is either in the middle kitchen drawer or in the hall closet.

In between is our furniture, our food and our beds which tend to stay pretty much where they belong.

But one time I was reading one of those articles on how to increase your efficiency. I'm always reading things like that for some reason. And this particular piece gave me a bad case of "Housewives' Guilt," I don't get the disease often, but when I do…

This time, in my frenzy of, "Housewives' Guilt" I put everything away. The hammer and tools went down to the tool box, and the bag of kitty litter that was on the chair with them went into the litter box to the astonishment of the cats.

For the first time in heaven knows when I say the table by the front stairs and the chair by the basement steps. The place looked absolutely unfurnished without our worldly goods waiting to be carried up or down as the case may be.

Did they notice? Yes, there was a reaction. It reminded me of that scene in Snow White and the Seven Dwarfs right after Snow White had come to the house of the dwarfs and cleaned it all up. She swept the floor, washed the dishes and put them in the cupboards.

When the dwarfs came home, Dopey looked around the spotless kitchen and whispered in a panic, "Our dishes have been stole." And Doc replied, "They ain't stole, they's been hid…in the cupboard."

Girl-child came home from school and eyed the clean hall table with dismay. "Our jeans," she wailed. "They've been ripped off." "They haven't been ripped off," said her brother, disgustedly. "Mother hid them upstairs in your closet."

"Oh yes, and the hammer is downstairs in the tool box," I added quickly before Himself reached the chair by the basement steps.

Home decorating difficult

In addition to being haunted, the house on Brown Street had funny windows. There were 32 of them, all either too wide or too tall for any ready-made curtains of the kind we could afford.

For a while we made do with curtains that were either two inches short or an inch or two narrow. The gap increased when they were washed. We knew this and rarely washed curtains.

What happens when you live in a very large house and shop in a world which manufactures for the three bedroom ranch with attached garages? Home furnishings had a way of diminishing once I got them in the house on Brown Street. I always suspected that they shrank in the car or something.

One way or another we managed to curtain all of the windows except for those in our own bedroom which were the funniest windows I have ever seen. Three casement windows, they were, swinging inward and so high you had to stand on a chair to look out. The room was about 9 feet wide and 18 feet long, with 10 foot ceilings. (I did say the house was odd, didn't I?)

The previous owners had left behind venetian blinds which I determined to get rid of right away. All this is by way of beginning to tell you the story of our bedroom curtains.

"Why don't we live here awhile until we are sure of what we want," suggested Himself. He always says things like this when faced with an insolvable problem.

"That's a good idea," I agreed. "I'll start looking around when I'm out shopping." I always say things like this when I can't figure out what to do either.

Friday night was shopping night, our big evening out. We brought groceries and visited the discount store for odds and ends.

"Maybe we'll pick up some curtains for the bedroom, while we are out there," we'd agree hopefully.

Usually we bought tennis shoes. A payday never passed that someone in the family didn't need tennis shoes. We must have bought several hundred thousand pair. Somewhere a chap sneakers company had grown wealthy because of us.

We bought nose drops and aspirin. You can't raise a family without nose drops and aspirin. And there were the light bulbs. My husband has this thing about light bulbs and has always been afraid we'd run out.

Finally we bought the toys. Every week we had to buy a cheap toy for every child in the house. This was the blackmail we paid so they'd let us out once a week without them. And then we'd walk by the curtain counter. Nobody who designs readymade curtains for discount stores ever heard of three casement windows higher than your head.

Neither did the decorating magazines we picked up at the magazine counter. "Get rid of those ugly old venetian blinds that are no longer in style," they'd recommend. And I'd retort, "What! And have the neighbors go upstairs and look into our bedroom and find out that I only make the bed when I think company is coming over?"

The magazine had nothing to reply to this, being written for people, who made beds on other days too. So we came home without bedroom curtains.

We moved from the house on Brown Street in 1972 and never did buy curtains for the bedroom. I was careful not to touch the venetian blinds which must have been hanging there for 30 years and were probably a little rotten by then. But I hoped the next tenants might think of something to do about them.

I was never able to find out if they did or not. I do know this: 22 years is a long time to go without bedroom curtains.

Home's Décor: "Big Catholic Family"

We bought some new furniture last month. In this affluent age I can hear everyone saying, "So what else is new, everybody buys furniture." But we aren't everybody.

For years our home was furnished in a style which could only be called "Big Catholic Family." It was a style no notable for decorator chic to say the least. What it was notable for was its supreme durability dirt resistant qualities and capaciousness.

A living room furnished in Big Catholic Family always had a kind of pro-tem appearance. Our living room looked as if we were just using a few old things people gave us to tide us over until the new furniture arrived. Naturally I never did much to discourage the thought.

Today I looked at my wing back chairs done in pale blue and grass green plaid. This would have been unthinkable when our color scheme was not even distinguishable. Pale blue would have been helpless under the onslaught of nine children and their six friends apiece.

Gone from our living room forever, lord help us, is the pillow and blanket on the couch. Someone was always sacked out there, home from school with a cold. Also gone and not missed are the empty baby bottles on the end table, the soggy sleepers abandoned by the armchair and jacks hiding in the carpet waiting to wound unsuspecting barefoot people on their way to the bathroom in the middle of the night.

Now I can buy pictures for the living room at a gallery instead of waiting until the children won them for selling Holy Childhood stamps from door to door. They also brought home numerous art objects, usually plastic statues of the Infant of Prague awarded for doing well in school. At one time I owned more plastic statues of the Infant of Prague than anyone I ever knew.

A bathroom done in Big Catholic Family was never free of piles of damp towels in the corner and there was always an overflowing diaper pail under the sink, a stern reminder of my current mission in life.

The kitchen's focal point was the table at which we fed the multitudes, performing daily the miracle of the loaves and the little fishes and tried to keep the dishes washed.

At this point if you are expecting an expression of longing for the good old days and a replay of Big Catholic Family, forget it. Did you ever hear anything Hercules said about wishing he could go back and do the stables again?

Middle age is filled with goodness if one is wise enough to see them, not the least of which is knowing one is past childbearing age and able to buy new furniture after 24 years.

We're here someplace – trapped in a jean heap

The other day I was complaining to a friend about my heavy work schedule; you know, the one where I work all day at the office and then moonlight as a cleaning lady (my own).

And then the friend, if I can still call her that, said, "You mean you do all that yourself? What've you got all those big strong kids for?"

"Now that you ask," I replied, "I'll have to think a minute. Actually, the reason I've got all those big strong kids is because I'm Catholic and God sent them to me because He liked me better than He likes a lot of other people. He did not, it appears, send them to me to help with the housework."

And this is why I have occasion to envy friends who tell how they've divided up the chores, having providentially trained their young from puppyhood to make beds and wash dishes before they toddle off to nursery school. Why them and not me?

Evidently God didn't send THEM children, He sent them housecleaners. At our house we already had one: me. My excuse has always been that when they were tots, I was too busy in the production department to get involved in employee training.

"Wouldn't it be nice if WE had a nice clean house like Billy Smith's," I used to ask, having heard children needed to care. Mine didn't.

"No," they'd reasoned, "Because if we did it'd mean we'd have to vacuum and wash woodwork all day like Billy."

I tried the calendar method. This looks great on a calendar. On target it doesn't work out, though it does impress friends viewing it stuck on the refrigerator. As soon as days for chores are scheduled, everyone changes practice time.

I've mentioned this before. Have you noticed that every youngster in the nation over the age of 5 has to go someplace after school to "practice?" Have you ever wondered what it is they're practicing for? The overthrow of the government, maybe?

I am sure that if my children had been Egyptians, they'd have found some way to get the pharaohs to build their own pyramids. But you have to hand it to the Egyptians. The only thing their kids ever got to practice was how to push granite uphill with a little help from their friends.

It probably took the place of dancing, gymnastics, band, piano, football and basketball practice all rolled (uphill) into one. Not only that, it kept the kids off the streets, and out of trouble and in great condition. History does not, though, record the hernia rate among Egyptian children.

But back to housework. Having discovered that wading through McDonald wrappers and jeans, while screaming doesn't work; I've resorted to the posting of threatening notes on the refrigerator. Often ignored by the children, these notes are a great source of entertainment to guests who like them even better than the calendar.

"Joe, take out those 18 plastic bags of junk, or suffer the consequences. They could grow into a garbage monster and eat us all. Signed, The Black Claw."

Or: "Holly, before you leave for band practice, practice your living room vacuuming. Remember the old saying, 'A woman is judged, not by her brains, but by the lint on her living room floor. (My mother-in-law).' Signed, your housecleaning coach."

Or: "Barb, load the dishwasher. Remember, cleanliness is next to Godliness and not only that, we've run out of paper plates and there is nothing left to eat dinner on, let alone fix it in. The wolf of starvation lurks at our messy door. Signed, Anxious Hungry Cook."

And failing all else, one day someone will find this note on the refrigerator, if they can find the refrigerator:

"Help! Whoever reads this note! My children and I are trapped somewhere in this mountain of jeans, dirty towels and half the unwashed jeans in town. We only have enough Coke and potato chips to last for a few hours. Signed, Desperate." (You remember; the one who was too busy in the production department to work on personnel training.)

It's like a jungle in kids bedroom

An all points office memo drifted across my desk last week. It was a suggestion to keep desks and surrounding areas clear of unnecessary paper. It was also a memory jogger of a time when my children's bedrooms were in such bad condition we toyed with the idea of abandoning them and hiring a bulldozer to push that wing of the house underground.

If fire marshals and federal officials are upset with what they feel to be an unreasonable amount of paper on top of desks, have they ever undertaken a concerted drive to clean up the rooms of children between the ages of 4 and 16?

I was having a cup of coffee one day with my neighbor, old Jane the Magnificent (the one who makes decorator furniture out of old egg cartons), and she said with the air of the one who prides herself on her parenting, "I insist that my children clean their own rooms."

To which I replied, "I agree. No mother in her right mind would venture into a child's room alone. Who knows what evil lurks under that pile of dirty socks? For years now, the kids have been telling me there's a monster in their room. They could be right."

I'm not saying I never cleaned one of those precious little kids' bedrooms: yellow ruffles and bows for girls; red, white and blue football helmets for boys. I did. But please notice a thing of two about those adorable children's bedrooms in decorating magazines.

Only rarely do you see a child in one. And even when there is a child, the magazine is careful to point out it's a model. You wouldn't dare put a live child in one of those rooms.

Putting a child in a newly decorated bedroom all his own is like dropping a tropical plant into a rainforest. Before you know it, he and his will have overgrown everything in sight. Like an evil creeping vine, the revolting stuff of which childhood is made takes over and covers the place from ceiling to floor.

Before you know it, the plush carpet is ankle deep in dirty socks which fill the air with their perfume. Jeans and discarded clothing cover most of the furniture. Posters, school papers and anything that you can drive a nail through and stick on a wall block a view of the designer wallpaper.

One in a while you'll hear the "children's telephone" ringing.

Don't bother looking for it. Only the children know where they last buried the phone, and it won't be for you anyway.

Also, not only do I advise you never to venture in there yourself, I've learned there's another good rule to remember. If you must go in, don't make the mistake of setting anything down. Whatever it is lurking under those hills of dirty clothes will dart out with a suction cup tentacle and slurp it up before you can scream, "Clean your room or you're grounded for a week."

Kids' rooms are a dilemma. No parent in his or her right mind would consider cleaning one unassisted. At the same time, a child's idea of cleaning up a room is to stuff everything in sight into drawers and under the bed. Leftovers are placed on the bed and decently covered with a spread.

Meanwhile, the room is presentable if you squint and hold your nose, but some things have disappeared completely, not to emerge until the child marries or leaves for college.

Usually we tended to look upon the children's rooms as areas to be quickly closed before we answered the doorbell and admitted any strangers.

Actually, I never called them the children's rooms. They were usually referred to as dens, lairs, caves, or pits. I wasn't very efficient, but I was realistic.

Chapter 9: Pets

You never know when you might need a cage

One time somebody gave us two rabbits. "Every child should have a pet,' somebody said as he presents us with a box containing to baby bunnies. Helps kids develop a sense of responsibility."

"That's what I hear," I muttered putting the bunny box on top of the refrigerator out of the way of two frantic toddlers and a dog gone suddenly insane. I remembered the pregnant cat we'd adopted once and the tame field mouse and the wild parakeet. How responsible are kids supposed to be.

Well nothing brings out responsibility in a parent like a package of rabbits. We couldn't keep them in that box forever. Rabbits grow, like all critters. Immediately the head of the house decided that our most important responsibility was a rabbit pen.

It was winter and we couldn't build an outdoor pen in the basement because the house had been built I in 1859, and the basement would frequently flood with three inches of water during the rainy season. That left the back room. A neighbor told us it had once been a kitchen, now it was just a catchall room with what turned out to be the first automatic dryer in the neighborhood, a washer and dirty laundry. Still room for a rabbit pen.

Himself bought what I thought was enough lumber to build a small house, some chicken wire and assorted nails and hinges. I told myself, "He's a guy. He knows how to build a rabbit pan. But I didn't really believe what I told myself, but I didn't say anything.

Every night after dinner, he'd head out to the back room with his sons to work on the pen. Every day I cleaned out the box of bunnies. The bunnies spent their time growing and growing.

"What are you going to put in that thing, Bengal tigers?" I asked my husband, as I walked around the vast new bunny house."

"They're already outgrowing their box and they'll need the space to exercise," he replied.

"We could take the whole family camping in it," I said.

He was miffed, I knew. "Look," he said. I don't criticize the way you clean the house. You don't knock my carpentry, OK?"

A son got into the discussion. "I don't think we'll be able to move it outdoors in spring," he observed, climbing in and standing upright. "Hey, this is neat. We could make a fort."

"Yes, we will, Himself told his son. "Now everyone clear out of here so I can put my tools away and get the pen ready. I'm sorry I ever offered to build the darn cage. There are lots of other things I could be doing, you know."

We tactfully left the room as he got busy reducing the hutch to half its original size so we could move it into the garage. Finally he finished, stocked it with straw, water and rabbit food. He didn't smile when I told him the whole thing reminded me of a story my dad told me once about a friend who build a boat in his basement and couldn't get it out. Until his children grew up they'd go downstairs to read or play they were at sea or watch one of the new television sets.

A few weeks later we gave the rabbits back to the rabbit giver. The cage? We stored it in a corner of the garage, figuring that one of these days we might need a cage again. We never did.

It's risky to keep "VIP" guinea pig

High on the list of the hurdles of motherhood is the day your 6-year-old comes home from school and announces: "Friday it's my turn to take the kindergarten guinea pig home for the weekend."

I let a kindergartener bring home the class guinea pig once, back when I didn't know any better. Now, when I even hear a small child say the words "guinea pig" I get the same panicky feeling I'd get if someone rushed in the house crying, "There's a seven foot tidal wave rushing up the street and you don't have a boat."

It is one matter to have your own guinea pig. After all, you paid for it and it's yours. The kindergarten guinea pig, on the other hand, is owned jointly by 35 six-year-olds, a teacher, and for all you know, funded by the federal government through a special project which provides guinea pig to kindergartens. No small responsibility.

Signing the note to let your little one take home the kindergarten guinea pig is not a project to be approached with levity and lightheartedness. Approach it rather as Eisenhower approached the invasion of Europe.

I signed the note in all innocence. The guinea pig came to visit and the first night under our roof it died. It wasn't killed by the cat or strangled by the baby. Tiny, whose name is etched on my soul forever, simply turned up his tiny toes and kicked the bucket sometime in the night, of natural causes.

The kindergartener was all for running away to be a cowboy once he'd stopped crying and began wondering what his teacher would say. We spent Saturday running around trying to replace Tiny, but the pet shops were fresh out of guinea pigs.

"It's your fault," said Himself, who always likes to think things are somebody's fault. "I can't imagine what you were thinking of when you consented to let him bring that darn thing home from school."

"How was I was going to know it would die the minute we got it in the house?" I asked him.

"You should have known that if Tiny was going to die this would be the place he'd pick to do it," he replied. "We're doomed that way."

As it turned out we didn't have to leave town or give ourselves up to the federal government. "It's perfectly all right," said the principal on the phone "The school has a special fund for such contingencies."

It was reassuring to know but that was the last time anyone around here ever got to bring the kindergarten guinea pig home from school.

Tale of the squirrel who came to dinner

To catch a squirrel you run around acting like a nut. To get rid of an old washing machine you catch a squirrel. And thereby hangs a tail…I mean a tale.

By means known only to rodents a squirrel got into the basement last fall and set up housekeeping in the cold air vents. I first met him one morning, going down the basement. He jumped from some shelves, hopped over my foot and sped down the stairs. That same night, when we thought the cat had finally chased him out, Himself went down and bricked up the hole where we thought the squirrel had come in.

We didn't know that we had walled our friend in for winter…just as he planned. We soon knew he was down there because when we watched TV at night he'd poke his nose through the cold air register and watch us. The kids were enchanted and rewarded him for his cleverness by poking all of their peanut butter crusts through the grate.

So that he – and we – wouldn't be frightened by each other we took to knocking loudly before entering the basement door which opens off the TV room. This warned the squirrel we were coming and also furnished a lot of entertainment for any guests who happened to be sitting there wondering why we always knocked on our basement door.

A survey of cold air ducts showed that he had stored piles of chestnuts there, filched from the collection the children put down the cellar last September. It was indeed the Conrad Hilton of the squirrel world.

"What's that noise?" startled visitors asked as he thundered through the air bents. "Oh, that's just the squirrel," we'd say, trying to act if it was something everybody had. "We don't know how to get rid of him." Somebody suggested poison, but everybody here was too tender hearted to consider such a crime. There had to be a kinder way to get rid of the Squirrel Who Came to Dinner.

We had it. One cold day we opened the back door, uncovered the register and coaxed the squirrel as far as the porch. He took one look at the snowbound outdoors and just refused to leave. We got nasty. So did he. Then when we were off guard he dashed into an old washing machine which had been sitting in the corner of the room since last fall. We hadn't been able to get that outside either.

He was trapped at last. Using muscle and brains we moved the squirrel, washing machine and all into the back yard. We had finally outwitted him.

The children wept buckets. "He'll die out there. He's never had to look for food." I'll go along with that. And it seemed a shame.

Still, as my husband says (he's the conservative in the family), "But good grief. Nobody keeps a squirrel in the register. What will people think?" He's right of course. It is unusual. But I can't help wondering what the squirrel thought.

Pyewacket Treated Like People

"You're certainly not going to let some pesky cat run our lives are you?" Himself asked as he watched me rummaging in the refrigerator.

"Oh, of course not," I replied. "But The Cat's a little off his feed and we can't let him starve, can we?"

"Can't we?" his tone implied that if He were Me there'd be no question about The Cat eating cat kibbles and table scraps. I'll go along with that. But it was a shame he had to be hanging around the kitchen while all this was going on.

I wouldn't say The Cat runs Old House. But last winter we left a screen with a big hole in it on an upstairs window because this was the way The Cat made his entrance and nobody wanted him to freeze out on the roof. Summer came and the bats came in so we had to replace the screen. Now when The Cat meows someone goes upstairs and unhooks the screen for him. For a cat he seems to have a might strong personality.

He only likes one kind of food, canned chicken parts. When he tires of this, which is often, he varies his diet with hamburger he cons out of me or any leftover roast or steak I can find. He detests fish and doesn't know that traditionally cats like milk. He won't touch it.

There is a serious population explosion of tiger kittens in the area and The Cat is their father. He bears a few of the battle scars common to tomcats, mostly because he is too lazy to fight. He does enjoy standing on his hind legs to snarl at passing felines. However The Cat and I understand each other so I never put him outside. He talks a good scrap and knows I won't embarrass him by calling his bluff.

The Cat was once gravely ill with a kidney infection and while he was at the veterinary hospital we realized what an important member of the family he was. We solemnly vowed that when The Cat came home there would be nothing too good for him. When he did come home our financial investment in him was so large we couldn't afford to let anything happen to him.

The Cat only comes when you call him politely by his given name which is "Pyewacket". The children say this is because he doesn't know he is a cat. How could he know, having been treated like people (royal people, in fact) for all of his three years. But he loves us dearly and happily consoles anyone who is sad by rubbing their tears with his whiskers. And I am the only woman in town with a giant tiger cat for a dining room table centerpiece. It's different. We love The Cat. But sometimes I think it would be cheaper to maintain a large Bengal tiger.

Looking for Luv in the Neighbor's Bushes 1968

There was an August moon in the sky when I crawled under the neighbors bushes. "Mind telling us what you are doing?" asked the friendly neighbor across the street as he watched from his porch. "As it happens, I'm looking for L.U.V."

I could hear him raising his eyebrows in the dark. "That," he said "is not the way to spell love. And why do you think you'll find it in Kelly's bushes? Himself is sitting right over there on your own porch."

"Kelly's bushes are as good a place to look for Luv as any," said I picking a barberry thorn out of my knee and gathering up Luv, our new tiger kitten. My neighbor went back to sitting on his porch. "Sometimes writers act kind of funny," he said to his wife. She nodded. "I knew what you mean."

Luv met us while we were at Houghton Lake and just insisted on becoming part of the family along with Goliath the mouse, Henry, the turtle and Bonnie and Clyde, the goldfish. Pyewacket, our big old tom cat, left us one March night and never returned. Luv, we felt, would be exactly the kitten to take his place. But as for renaming him Pye, well somehow, we just couldn't see him as anything but Luv.

"But it's going to sound silly, yelling "Here Luv", every time we call him." said various members of the family. "Yeah, let's have mother call him. She never feels silly."

When I came home with Luv, I told Himself about my conversation with the neighbor man. He was not amused. "It's the stupidest name for a cat I ever heard anyway. Maybe we'd better just call him Kitty. If you go running out every night telling the neighbors you can't find love, someone is going to call the law on you."

I agreed. Luv should have a new name. Just then the kitten jumped off my lap and headed down the street and behind a house. I ran after him. "Excuse me," I said to the woman who answered the door. "Do you mind if I climb your tree. I'm trying to find Luv." She raised her eyebrows and then shrugged. "Go ahead if you think you'll have any luck."

Luv clung to a branch far out of reach. Someone once told me never to worry if a cat climbed a tree. The always come down when they get hungry. Luv didn't look a bit hungry. "Get down from there you rotten little beggar," I snarled. Luv didn't say anything. He climbed a few feet higher.

I went home without Luv. Tomorrow I thought he'll either come when I yell 'Kitty Kitty' or he can stay away. Next morning he was home. "Hi, Kitty" I said opening his cat food. "Mother, his name is Luv," said all the children.

The magic of Luv

As of today we still have our middle-size, not too bright tiger cat named Luv, the one I made neighborhood history with by calling his name under the neighbor's bushes. To us there is no more beautiful, intelligent or clever cat in the world.

But he didn't wind a single prize in the recreation department pet show last summer. He wasn't the biggest, smallest, prettiest or smartest. In the eyes of the judges he was the most nothing animal there. In the sight of his adoring family there is no other cat around who can match him, and when he goes away and we replace him with another striped cat it won't be the same somehow.

We know, because there has never been another Pyewacket, the cat with thumbs that Joe was sure had previously belonged to a witch. He thought this because at night Pye would arch his back and look mean. Pyewacket was undoubtedly a different type of cat. Totally lacking in personality he slept under the couch during the day, emerging only to eat and leave promptly at 10 p.m.

One night he left forever and you would have thought a brother vanished. Oh the grieving: the days we spent asking around the area if puzzled residents had seen a big striped cat with thumbs, the only one in captivity.

For a year it was rumored among the neighbors that a mean looking cat with thumbs was raiding local garbage cans and battling with other toms, but after a bit the rumors died down, and we began looking for, if not another Pye, at least a cat to fill the cat-gap in our home.

Then along came Luv whose only claim to being special is that he doesn't have a 'meow' and is afraid to go out alone after dark. But to his owners he is an extraordinary being who quite understands when children lie and tell him that a 10-cent can of cat food really costs 30 cents, because he won't eat anything he thinks is bargain food.

Like doting parents who dearly love a plain, unaccomplished only child, or a bride madly in love with her nondescript, middle-size husband who will never set the world on fire; like all who love, Luv's owners have spun a glowing halo of all that is beautiful and good around a creature who wouldn't be much without it.

This is what love does to almost anything. You see a child, a woman, an animal, a garden or a racing car. Then we see them through the eyes of somebody who loves them, someone who will point out all of the special little things about them nobody ever noticed before.

A lot of people and things are like this. They only need someone who cares about them to show the world what it may have been missing all along. Luv may not have been much of a cat to the judges in the pet show, but to those who meet him through our eyes, he is a cat of some renown and great character.

The night they stole the cat - Luv threatened by cat-nappers

It was just twilight and Holly just happened to look the window in time to see three youngsters scoop up a cat from the sidewalk as they passed the house.

"Somebody's stealing Luv," she screeched at the top of her lungs, and hordes of Hansens poured out the front door. "What's wrong? Is your house on fire?" asked some kids playing across the street.

"Somebody's stealing Luv," yelled all of the Hansens as they ran up Brown Street after the three kids carrying the cat, who by had realized they were being pursued and started running.

"Don't worry, we'll get him back." Said the kids playing across the street and joined the posse.

Three high school girls talking to three high school boys on somebody's front porch hollered, "What's wrong" an accident?"

"Those kids running up the street just stole Hansen's cat," yelled back the thundering herd which was growing by the block. A neighbor man shoveling his walk stepped aside. "A fire?"

"Somebody's stealing Hansen's cat." hollered the still growing crowd.

The man jumped in his car. "I'll catch him for you." was the gallant offer. By now the cat stealers had put a block and a half between them and their pursuers.

At the corner of Brown and Holland Avenue the cat-nappers were stopped by the man in the car. "But we didn't steal the cat. This is our cat, they said, producing a black and white cat on a turquoise leash.

What does a mob of 20 angry neighbors chasing three cat-nappers say to three cat-nappers who aren't?

Beyond profuse apologies, nothing. Slowing the crowd returned to their homes.

"Well, it could have been the Hansen's cat," said a couple of the kids.

"The man in the car was not available for comment. He went right in the house and no one saw him for a day or two.

"Yeah, Holly," said all of the Hansen's, "How come you couldn't tell a striped cat from a black and white cat on a leash?"

Clearly Holly felt threatened by her relatives. "But it was dark out. And it could have been Luv."

"That's right," everybody agreed. "It could have been."

Luv had nothing to say. He'd been asleep on the stereo out in the back room and missed all of the excitement. It was probably just as well.

The Cat That Isn't

Why did I ever think that cats eat mice and drink milk? Of course it isn't so strange. I was also one who believed, until recently, that mice loved cheese and rabbits lived on lettuce.

Luv, the Houghton Lake orphan, who has been with us for six years now, does not eat mice. His soul brother, Black Sabbath, isn't above catching an occasional mouse and he would have been much appreciated when we lived in the old house on Brown Street.

Our old house was popularly known, among mice, as the Holiday Inn of the rodent world. Mice came and went there, helped themselves to our food and wood and gobbled up unmouselike quantities of insulation.

It was only natural that boy mice would meet girl mice cavorting in the labyrinths of our walls, and that a certain amount of cohabitating would take place with the usual results. Baby mice abounded, as we'd discover on moving a stove or shoring up a crumbling piece of plaster.

Most of the time the mice lived better than we did and didn't even have to pay taxes for it. There is no crime in mouseville, we never had a mouse mugged on our property, something we couldn't say for a few of our neighbors.

Most important of all, mice never had to live in fear of a cat. Not that we didn't have a cat, we did. We had Luv, who ate only the finest cat food, and only when it wasn't on sale, never indulged in a bowl of milk and never caught a mouse.

I used to think cats went crazy when they saw mice run across the floor. Luv didn't even turn his head. We tried everything, including catching a mouse and giving it to him. But he turned up his whiskers and went to stand by his dish, waiting for his half a can of Cat Gourmet, the expensive brand.

And all the time we had a wall full of baby mice who were growing up thinking cats were things that sat and stared at baby mice when they toddled across the living room floor.

The children helped the mice by making paper tables which they left behind the pantry door (the entrance to the mouse motel) filled with bits of cheese and graham cracker.

At night we listened to the scratching behind the walls, or caught a glimpse of a mouse watching us from the cold air register and realized we had to fight the mice unaided.

Well, not entirely unaided. We set traps, which we bated with the cheese and put behind the door in place of the little tables. This meant rising before dawn so the children wouldn't discover their parents were killers of mice. Luv couldn't have cared less.

One day I was telling a new acquaintance about the problem of ridding a century-old house of mice. "We'd call an exterminator," I said, "but we don't want the children to know we are getting rid of our mice."

"I know what you need," she said wisely. "Get yourself a cat. It'll finish those mice in a jiffy."

"So they say," I said sadly. "We've got something resembling a cat now. But from your description I've concluded that's not what Luv really is."

Go gentle into the night

Luv is dead. Our family cat. He of the soft stripped fur and the face of a giant kitten died Wednesday afternoon, and with him died a large portion of our family experience. He was 10 years old.

We cried together, and our friends who love cats cried with us. And to people who do not even own a pet, the sight of our tear-stained faces probably did seem ridiculous. "It isn't as if a person died," someone said.

Perhaps it is ridiculous to grieve so much for a small dumb creature. But what dies with a beloved pet are those scenes of our lives in which he played a part. And Luv was indeed a decade of our children's growing up.

Thinking of him I see my young son on the beach at Houghton Lake, remembering how he talked daddy into letting him bring that skinny, scraggly little stripped kitten back to Saginaw. "We've named him Luv, "He said.

I remember the awful silver Christmas tree that revolved as a built-in music box played "Silent Night." Luv, always discerning about life, shared my dislike of the monstrosity. Each year he attacked it regularly and fiercely until the grids of the music box were silenced and the three no longer turned. Thanks to Luv we bought a new tree.

"But cats are so useless," my husband was fond of saying when one the girls walked around the house wearing Luv around her neck like a fur piece. "All they do is eat and sit around and ask to be let outside. "But which of God's creatures does so little with exquisite class?" I've always reminded him. "Could anything else be so useless and still be so cherished?"

And cherished he was. The children lavished mountains and waterfalls of affection on him from the day we found him up north, a hopeless orphan. Whoever brings stray kittens home from a resort?

We took him out to the veterinary clinic Sunday night, so ill he didn't care where he was going, no uneasy meows, no anxious looks out of the car window, no problems. Nothing but the small furry body lying listlessly across my daughter's lap.

He had a lot to live for and stayed alive for four more days. But he wasn't strong enough to fight the infection which raged in his lungs causing him to fight for each breath he could catch. He died in a coma, and with him died a family epoch.

We buried Luv under a lilac tree belonging to a friend who loves cats and understands. She planted some baby chrysanthemums for a marker. There is no place to bury a pet when you live in a rented townhouse.

But mighty kings and princes die, and so do small cats, making death seem but a slight problem shared by all creatures. Losing a loved one falls gently, if sadly, into its proper perspective.

And yet, I'm one of these people who always hopes forever. I want to keep my golden times unchanged, and I look back wistfully when they fade and disappear into the time behind.

Luv died. All things die. I am reminded again that nothing is faster than the speed of time, and life is indeed a loving gift to be lovingly lived.

So, go gentle into that good night, little friend. I will miss you.

Chapter 10: Vacation and travel

Successful family vacation takes courage

It takes a certain type of woman to vacation successfully with small children. She must be calm, well organized and courageous, the type who could fight Indians on the Nebraska plains without blowing it. I also helps greatly if she is not pregnant.

I am not this type of woman which accounts for the fact that over the years we have vacationed poorly and seldom. There was this time we went camping. Every morning Himself would say cheerfully, "I'll wander down to the beach for a while and get out of your way so you can get things in order. Then we can really relax and enjoy ourselves."

While he wandered I boiled bottles, made formula, fed and bathed the baby, swept the tent and made beds. I hauled water a quarter of a mile through dense forest and got lunch. Himself returned. "Well, what do you want to do today?" he'd ask. "Watch the baby. I'm going to bed," I'd say falling on the nearest cot.

Much later he told an acquaintance who asked about our camping trip, "Oh we didn't do much of anything. All I did was watch the baby while Betty slept. But she got a good rest anyway."

Then there was the time we rented a cottage. Herb Jr. was just starting to toddle. "It says in the ad that the beach is only 75 feet away. That means we can lie around in the sun all day and let the baby play in the water." I'll say this for my husband; he starts out with high hopes anyway. The water was indeed 75 feet from the cottage…straight down. We spent a miserable week preventing our son from falling into it, something he tried valiantly to do every waking minute.

Another time we went fishing and were kept company by numerous dragonflies the size of ducks that landed on the boat seat and kept staring at me with all six eyes. They had evidently never seen a pregnant fisherman before. Himself acted as if he'd always known duck-sized dragonflies and hardly noticed. But I have a thing about bugs. We finally had to go to shore because my shrieks were drawing a crowd on the dock wondering if I'd gone into labor out in the middle of the lake.

"I'll never take you fishing again as long as I live," muttered my husband as we strode by the gawking resorters. "You're darned right you never will." I replied.

Time has passed and old wounds have healed and we have decided to risk it once again. The baby is going on eight and surely this year we can have the kind of vacation you see on cigarette commercials. Anyway we are still living in hope. Houghton Lake here we come.

Our summer vacation

One Sunday morning we loaded our nine cardboard cartons, three suitcases, the supermarket sacks and the cooler into the car. Truly we did. Between the carrier on top and the trunk we somehow managed to pack all of our supposed dire necessities into the auto and then stood back wondering if it would still hold the family without bursting its tires.

It had to. So with a prayer on our lips we headed for America's Playground with the car riding like a speedboat, rear nearly touching the road and the front tilted upward. Expressways on Sunday resembled those carnival rides where all the little cars see how close they can come to ramming each other without actually making it. But this is not game. Clearly the highway is not place for the meek, nor is it a place for those not in a state of grace.

There is an evil gremlin who lives with us. I don't mean the one who loses all of the jar and bottle caps. This one devotes his life to doing whatever he can to making the Hansen vacations miserable as possible without actually brining us to anything drastic. And for a minute it seemed that our nasty little gremlin was out to get us again.

For when we arrived at our cottage we found there were no screens on our screened-in porch. The reason, we were informed, was that there was a nest of baby birds out there and no one could screen in the porch until they were old enough to leave.

Well you can't come right out and say, nevertheless you paid for a screened in porch and feel you should have it. Because not loving birds is like being against motherhood and patriotism and think of what St. Francis would say besides. So I took a couple of pills widely advertised on TV for women's tension headaches and fumed to myself.

Besides there were the nine cardboard boxes, three suitcases, the supermarket sack and the cooler still waiting in our exhausted automobile.

It is amazing though how quickly a family can stow its gear, choose up bedrooms and get dressed for the beach.

Our vacation hideaway, built in 1922 was old-fashioned, uncomplicated and miles away from the commercial honkytonk, set in 19 acres of woods on the eastern shore of Houghton Lake. It was many windowed and swept by breezes from the shore. The beds and dressers all looked antique, but we had a brand new stove and refrigerator.

There was no telephone to call us from our thoughts and no TV to keep us from having any. "But what am I going to look at all day?" inquired the youngest when he found this out. In 10 minutes he found a hutch of rabbits up behind the big old lodge as well as two cats and a kitten. In less than an hour, lulled by the wind in trees and moving water the whole family began to unwind. We watched the mother bird feeing her young and never even missed the screened-in porch.

Chapter 11: St. Mary's

Dominican nuns, you have a fan

Happy Birthday, Dominican nuns at St. Mary's Cathedral. This being the anniversary of your 100th year in the service of the Lord, I'd like to share with you some of my private funny, nunny memories, interwoven as they were with my children growing up.

Your particular quality of majestic, intimidating other-worldliness was best summed up by one of my children. It was that day you swept down the cathedral aisle in your flowing black robe and white wimple and my three-year-old looked up with all the joy one would feel at such and encounter and said, "Hi, God."

I remember your voice on the phone. There was that distinctively modulated tone that said "Sister is calling," even before you gave your name. "It's a nun," reverently whispered my son, calling me to the phone. "You can tell by her voice."

You either did or did not believe that black patent shoes reflected up. But the legend provided the title of a best-selling book and much mirth among your budding female students. Your aim was to keep them pure and unsullied. Your average wasn't bad.

My mental view of you is of a black and white mosaic with increasing dashes of color as you discarded voluminous black habits and white wimples for polyester pantsuits and new hairdos.

I remember Sister James, the school principal, all 4-feet-10-inches of her. Standing on her faith, she looked 12-feet tall and her silent, unsmiling presence could quell playground riots.

Rosy-cheeked, round faced Sister Margaret, who without complaint taught 55 first graders to read. What's more they came out of their grade reading better than other children.

I remember the Halloween Day you decreed that each child should come to school dressed as the saint for whom he or she was named. Evidently your after-hours seclusion from the outside world left you shielded from big family realities.

"St. Ralph?" said my husband and I incredulously, when our son finally got around to giving us the command from school. But I came through for you. You knew I would, knowing also that I was scared to death of you and so was Ralph. On the basis of the concession (something you rarely made) that if the saint was impossible to duplicate, we could choose an alternative, I chose St. Jude, patron saint of the impossible.

St. Jude looked strangely like St. Joseph-left-over-from-the-Christmas-pageant. Still, you were nice enough not to notice, pointing out that even St. Jude probably had a change of clothes.

I watched you striding fearlessly into pagan lands, both here and overseas. I saw you marching for civil rights, speaking out with the courage of St. Joan, glorying in your post-Vatican II freedom like uncaged skylarks soaring heavenward.

Dominican nuns, I'm one of your biggest fans. I never assumed, as did many cradle Catholics, that you fell from the sky, clothed in black and white with unspotted souls. I admire you because you are, at once strong and weak, stable and a little nutty, spiritual and earthy. To this day, I can't try on a pair of the famed black patent shoes without wondering. You do manage to leave your imprint upon many, many souls. Have a great hundredth.

Parents, Son Awed by Sister

Occasionally you meet a teacher capable of inspiring immense respect in her students. It isn't anything she says or does exactly; it's just that she is sort of perfect. When our John was in second grade he had such a teacher. And when John came home from school dramatically prefacing a classroom edict with the ominous words, "Teacher said…" you can bet nobody around here ever argued. We were as awed by Teacher as John.

There was the Baby Science Fair. John announced at bedtime one evening that tomorrow was the Baby Science Fair. "And if I don't have a project in I'll get an F. Teacher said…" It wasn't clear why we had failed to hear about the Baby Science Fair sooner since it developed that other second grader had been working on a project for two weeks. But Teacher had spoken and there comes a time when it is too late to argue over trivialities like the breakdown in communication between home and school. So we set about trying to assemble a science project for John.

Someone facetiously suggested a butterfly collection. In the middle of March? And obviously it was too late to starve a mouse for a nutrition project. Finally the whole family began roaming about the house looking for something remotely scientific. In desperation I suggested that maybe John might have to get an F. But the look of speechless horror on his face put a stop to that argument.

Then I remembered the bouncing mothball trick where you put some citric acid and soda into water with some mothballs which rise and fall with chemical reaction. It was pretty and as scientific as we could get on such short notice. The drugstore supplied the chemicals, I furnished the instructions and by bedtime John had a project.

I hoped this would teach John a lesson of some sort and it did. He learned that id your mother does your project for you on the night before it is to be handed in you will get an A. So John brought home first prize, to our everlasting shame, and for a long time we had some odd ideas about Science Fairs. Teacher said I should have looked carefully for that notice she has sent home six weeks before. She was right, as always.

New awareness rises out of rude awakening

To the Class of 1969 of St. Mary's Cathedral High School on the occasion of your class reunion:

It was hard to think of something to say to you when you asked me to be your speaker. I still remember you as children: cute, bright, funny, unbelievable innocent, filled with hope and sure there was nothing about the big outside world you couldn't handle.

You were indeed among the last Catholics in America of whom author John Powers writes so touchingly. Black patent leather shoes really reflected up, and God stood by wearing a nun's habit, ready to strike you dead for some unintentional offense.

In many ways you haven't changed, though you are no longer children. The wisdom and pain of 10 remarkable years have left their imprint on your faces and in your eyes. By now you have witnessed or felt marriage, children, death or divorce. You have experienced love affairs, hirings, firings, college, successes, sorrow and joy.

You stepped, unsuspecting, from the sheltered world provided by your parents and church into a decade which ultimately changed practically everything you were ever taught.

The Vietnam War altered the way of the games of war played. No longer is anything done because it is "patriotic," or "because that's the way it's done," or because someone in authority decrees it.

Flower children blossomed in the dust of the drug culture, then wilted and died with their promises un-kept. Watergate proved that if Big Brother watches, you'd best be watching back, and nobody has trusted anybody in power since.

Up to this point, the last 10 years sound pretty dreadful. But there is a lighter side to the rude awakening. People have learned to live more comfortably with the differences between them.

There is a fresh appreciation of that which is genuine, personal creativity and openness to new experience. The "back to nature" movement, once left to the folks out in the communes, has become a class operation.

Ten years ago, who would have dreamed we could slice our vegetarian diet up in a $240 food processor and cook it in seconds in a $500 microwave oven? Or that running would replace sex as the most talked about sport in America.

Nor had we yet witnessed the amusing paradox of the pot smoker who insists upon herbal tea and avoids Twinkies because he doesn't want chemicals in his body; or watched home-made bread move from a domestic skill to an art form.

"I think we're happier now than we were then," commented one of you at the reunion. I believe this. Loss of innocence doesn't necessarily mean loss of joy. Rather it means a new awareness of how much there is to be joyful about.

It does seem to be your fate, though, to be stepping off into another hectic period of change. But you should be pretty good at it by now. Change is a part of your lives.

Supposedly, we are running out of energy, there's a recession up the road and on the way we'll have to duck falling Skylab. Yet, in the face of this, and beneath the wisdom you have acquired is the same good humor and hope in the goodness of mankind you had back in 1969.

I didn't tell you all of this in my speech because I didn't want to come to your class reunion and cry.

Chapter 12: Seasons and Holidays

There is a God...This is His world

You once asked me in a letter, "What do you believe? What is your philosophy of life?" So today, on Easter Sunday, I will try to answer.

I believe truly, there is a God, that this is his world and that He loves me and wants me in it. If He didn't I wouldn't be here. Also, since He does love and want me here, it stands to reason He loves everyone else who is here, so it follows that as one of His children I should do the same.

I didn't always think so, and looking back it is hard to recall when I first began to feel this way. At the end of the war I read about the pitiful skeletons who crawled or were carried from Nazi concentration camps and asked sadly, "How could He let this happen to those He loved?" Then someone told me how some of these prisoners, returning home had stopped by a shrine long enough to kiss the ground of their homeland and praise God for their liberation. They had loved and trusted Him in spite of much suffering, for they knew it was not he who denied them love but their fellow man.

Maybe it was a spring morning after a serious illness. Awakening to sunlight after a long time of pain and hopelessness, feeling the wonder of being alive still; the miracle of being able to see, to feel, to touch, to hear, and to speak and making a promise not to forget ever the simple glory of my own senses.

Or it could have been an early dawn after being up all night with a restless child, feeling exhausted, cross and sorry for myself, then hearing a bird's clear song through an open bedroom window. "You are never alone," it said to me.

And maybe this is why I do not always grieve when somebody old goes peacefully to death from a good and orderly life, but my heart will break for a young hoodlum killed in a gun battle with the police. His real tragedy was not that he wasn't loved, but that he never knew someone wanted him here in the world and had given him life with a promise of something much better.

This is indeed our Father's world and each of us is needed and wanted in it. Many people know this already, as do I, and have but to show by our own words and deeds those who do not know it that they are wanted also. "He prayeth best who loveth best all things both great and small. For the dear Lord who madeth us, He made and loveth all."

Rejoice and be glad my brothers! Easter morning has come to the house of Our Father.

Make no myth-stake, Easter Bunny is a She

The only people likely to be surprised by this revelation will be my children -- at least the ones who don't know by now.

This is spilling the jelly beans to be sure. But it's not that hard for me to understand children's faith in the Easter Bunny. After all, for years I WAS the Easter Bunny.

One Saturday morning two of the children, both of them under age 6, sat in front of the television speculating upon the character of the magic rabbit.

"I think he's taller than Dad and hops down the street carrying our baskets in his front paws," said one tot to his little brother.

"Where does he keep all the rest of the baskets?" asked the other. "He's only got two front paws."

"He gets them by magic. When he puts two baskets down, two more come and jump up on his paws. He never runs out."

They aren't even close, I reflected from my post at the dishwasher.

First off, the Easter Bunny (being me) was female. But not once did the children ever call the Easter Bunny "she."

And this business of baskets appearing by magic, my rabbit's foot. A lot of work when into those baskets of jelly beans and candy chicks -- a lot of money, too.

Take it right from the bunny's mouth -- the Easter Bunny works almost as hard and spends almost as much money as Santa.

Easter Sunday wasn't so bad. On a good one the children could have their baskets cleaned out and at least one boiled egg mashed into the carpet by breakfast.

Saturday was a big production day. I always believed it was best to boil and color the eggs after the little ones were asleep so they'd think the Easter Bunny produced them all by himself --, er, herself.

Hollow rabbits and full hearts

I must have been very little, not more than five or six, when my mother bought me an Easter dress of lavender voile with a matching taffeta slip. "The color of a beautiful fragrant flower," she told me, when I asked what lavender was.

It could have been the same year when I learned in school how to make my own Easter basket from green construction paper, mitered and pasted at the corners. That was the day we came in from recess to find our baskets filled with paper grass and candy eggs. Somehow the magic rabbit had found us in school.

Easter, like Christmas, was always a surprise. We never helped our parents color eggs. They just appeared on Sunday morning and were, we supposed, carried to our home by a seven-foot white rabbit who hopped quietly through the house with our baskets hanging from his forepaw.

But I had never gotten close enough to a chocolate rabbit to learn they were hollow. When I had children of my own I always bought them chocolate rabbits. One should find out about their hollowness early, I told myself.

I remember how the church smelled like flowers on Easter morning and the pews, slippery and shiny with new varnish. All of the blue and black and brown winter women who crowded into the seats around me blossomed into spring ladies of yellow, pink and pale green with flower-laden heads.

In later years I dressed my own children for Easter Sunday services; little plaid sport coats and white shirts and ties for the boys, tiny white gloves and white straw bonnets that tied under the chin for the girls.

Our sons would march in the Easter processions in high-collared red robes and starched cassocks. It seemed that Easter was for boys in those days. They got to sing in the choir, serve communion and follow the bishop around.

Girls wore their best dresses under pastel coats and had demurely covered heads. They sat in the pews and looked pretty. Their turn to shine would come in May with the crowning of the Blessed Virgin. Mary's processions were nearly always for girls only.

We were told that stuffed bunnies, yellow chicks and rainbow eggs were pagan symbols of the rites of spring and secretly felt a little guilty about our enchantment with all of these childish things we could not seem to put away. Year after year I continued to buy and enjoy these pagan symbols, do what I would.

I can't remember when all of these things faded from my life. We went to church as always on Easter morning and came home to a candy dish of jelly beans on the coffee table. There were no more believers at home. Nobody needed new clothes for Easter, or if they did they were able to buy their own.

Once I had worn a lavender dress to church and wished for a chocolate rabbit. And once I had stayed up late to color eggs for the morning when I watched my sons march the Easter procession.

I no longer feel guilty about buying pink stuffed bunnies and marshmallow chicks. Again I see Easter morning bathed in golden sunshine, smelling faintly of spring. There may be snow beneath my feet, but the ground where the crocuses lie sleeping is beginning to warm.

Around me all of nature rejoices in the fact that things grow and die and then return life again. Now my grandchildren wear new dresses to church and come home to their baskets of candy.

And I will celebrate again the sureness of infinity and the renewal of life.

Lenten memories

Remember the Lenten fast? It was a six week period during which people of certain faiths ate less than usual under the absurd notion that no making a pig of oneself every day in the year improved the character.

It began simply enough with the parish priest reading the Lenten regulations from the pulpit on the Sunday before Ash Wednesday, which today is, and why I am reminded of Lent. The Lenten rules required that the two light meals of the day shouldn't equal the main meal.

No meat on Ember Days or Fridays, meat only at the main meal of the day, and none at all on Fridays. Looking back, it doesn't sound like too much of an order. Any staunch Catholic could have done it and did, largely because Father managed to make the reading of the Lenten regulations sound like the recitation of the Articles of War.

Sundays were "live it up days' during the good old years. The guys who gave up beer for Lent, had their six packs all ready to go for Sunday when nobody had to fast.

Everybody at our house gave up something for Lent except me. This was because I was pregnant most of the time anyway, so I decided the Lord was providing me with all of the penance I needed.

Someone once accused me of managing to be in a family way every Lent so I wouldn't have to fast, which reminds me of people who think ADC mothers have babies to get pay raises. It just isn't worth it.

There were attending problems like sending a husband to work with a lunch pail filled with bologna sandwiches because you forgot the part about meal only once a day. If he was the easy going type he ate them anyway, but if he was super conscientious he came home from the shop half-starved and didn't speak for the rest of the evening, other than to accuse his wife of trying to send him to Hell.

Now people do not have to go through all this unless they wish it, and the new idea of Lent is to go forth and do lots of good works which is also a good idea. Except that now the only people who can really tell you what it feels like to do without and be hungry are the people for whom good works are being done.

For me the hard part of the Lenten fast came during those times when I wasn't expecting a baby and had to fast, and also fill six or seven Easter Baskets Holy Saturday evening.

Working with piles of candy, colored hard boiled eggs and chocolate bunnies during the Saturday "black fast" as we liked to call it then, was the final and worst penance of Lent.

But it was worth it when, at midnight, I got out of bed and sneaked out to the dining room table and at all the black jelly beans out of the kids' Easter baskets. Somehow I felt I had earned them.

Chapter 13: Christmas Memories

Christmas 1941 quiet beginning

There was absolutely nothing that night and day to herald all of the funny, spectacular, touching, noisy, unusual, sometimes lavish, sometimes skimpy, occasionally confusing Christmases as the Lord was to provide us. It stands to reason that when two people from two different backgrounds get married, there is a "how-do-we-celebrate Christmas" gap. There was.

December 1941 was historic. Pearl Harbor Day was less than three weeks behind us. The war I spent my teen years believing to be inevitable had arrived. Boys I dated before I was married never talked about the future in terms of future careers. Instead they spoke of "maybe, if I come back from the war." Dad was working at the Saginaw Steering Gear, which had already begun to manufacture parts for machine guns. Manufacturing plants in Saginaw, indeed, all over the country, were retooling for war materials. Rationing of gasoline, shoes and many food items were being organized. Newspaper and radio reports of the war, the draft and how our country was gearing up for massive warfare.

Still, there were things we didn't know about each other. One of them was how we perceived Christmas as a celebration. We agreed that since we were a family (almost), we should begin our own holiday traditions. So we bought a tiny table tree, piled our presents around it, turned off all the lights except those on the tree and began our first family Christmas.

At age 17, soon-to-be-18, I still missed my family. I missed hanging up stockings (which we still did, even my parents). I missed the quiet time when we read the Christmas story from the Bible, then tiptoed off to bed. I missed the fun of helping my parents put out the presents and toys for my younger brothers and sister. What I didn't know, until many years later, when Dad and I really did know each other well enough to talk about what was in our hearts, was that he suffered some regrets of his own.

As one of the youngest in a large family, he missed the Christmas Eve celebration in his folks big kitchen – the married brothers and sisters coming over with their children for a late supper and to exchange gifts they brought, having drawn names at the annual family Thanksgiving.

I hated the commotion he missed – the laughter, quarrels, the uncles having too much to drink, the aunts being properly indignant, the going home exhausted at three in the morning. He thought this was what Christmas was all about.

He didn't find our family Christmases at all exciting, wonder in fact, if there wasn't something sadly lacking in the Morningstar view of Christmas. Where were all the relatives on Christmas Eve?

There were none in Saginaw. An aging Aunt and Uncle and a Grandmother in a small town up in the Thumb area (of Michigan) – some relatives of Grandpa Morningstar's down in Ohio, occupied with families of their own – my parents, busy preparing a "dull" Morningstar-type Christmas for my young brothers and sister.

That first Christmas of ours found me extremely pregnant, uncomfortable and cross. A typically Michigan snowy, slippery, windy night was going on outdoors – hardly a night a pregnant young woman would go out in just for fun. Beside all this, we didn't have a car, which made deciding where we would spend Christmas Eve more of an academic decision than a choice.

So there you have it. Our very first Hansen Christmas – not particularly romantic, somewhat unmemorable except for someone like me who thinks practically everything that happens is memorable one way or another. It was also a scary time for me. I feared the mystery and pain of delivering a baby. I was afraid I might die in childbirth, afraid of becoming a war widow with a child to raise. I was afraid of my own inadequacy in all these situations.

If Dad was afraid of any of these things he didn't share his fears with me.

Christmas for Dad and I rarely approached story-book perfection. Christmases for us tended to be – well, weird somehow – nothing like the normal holidays other people seemed to be having.

When Santa went to war

By the time Herb's first Christmas rolled around, he was a week short of his first birthday. He had been walking since he was 10 months old, to the chagrin of his Grandmother Hansen, who had heard small babies walked early and big babies walked later.

Herb was a big baby – a big, big, big baby, in fact. I was warned that I really ought to do something to hold the kid back, so he wouldn't get bowlegged or knock-kneed or (I privately suspected) until his older Hansen cousins, who were born the same year, but were much smaller, could catch up.

But I didn't know how to hold back a large, walking baby, nor did Dad. Perhaps we should have had a talk with him about the un-wisdom of early walking, but when, at 11 months old, he was able to climb as high as the piano keys, it seemed a little late. He was already doomed to whatever fate met babies who walked "before their time." He could talk too.

World War II had taken over our very existence. Meat, sugar, fats, shoes and several other things I can't remember were rationed. Small families, like ours, had very meager supplies of stamps to buy these things. Occasionally a merciful relative or friend with an excess of coupons would donate some. Other times we could be really clever at making do.

It was the first of three wooden Christmases for Herb. Ralph came along in July of 1945, so missed out on wartime presents. Herb (we called him "Herbie" then) got lots of blocks that year, but all 11-month olds kids get blocks. He got a couple of wood pull toys, a toy with graduated wood rings piled one on top of another and a stuffed toy or two – not made of wood. They were made of materials I salvaged from old cotton clothing. Cotton and wool good were also scarce by then.

The second year, a friend of mine donated some beautiful steel trucks and cars she saved from her own boys' childhood. Dad took them apart and cleaned them, then repainted them, as only he could, in bright enamel so they looked as good as new.

Small children simply assumed all airplanes were bombers. They had to be, because grownups would look skyward at the formations going over our house from Wurtsmith Air Force base, and say, "Look at all those bombers."

Herb got toy wooden bombers for Christmas. I tried to draw the line on toy guns, but was more or less outgunned by Dad. So Santa brought Herb a wooded rifle and machine gun, painted military green. He also bought him a little soldier suit and a military hard hat. I don't recall that plastic has been invented yet. There were few, if any metal toys. It was probably made out of some sort of papier mache or composition.

Dad was working seven days a week in the "war plants" as they called them. Actually, he worked the second shift, which made for long winter nights for me – no doubt for him too, toiling away making machine guns.

He didn't have to go in the service. His asthma helped keep him out, plus as the war went on, he aged out of the draft, having been 27 when we were married.

I wasn't a war widow in the exact sense of the word. I was alone as much as one, however. But it had good points; I know how to be alone well, having developed inner resources during times like this. One thing I did was go to the library a lot. I'd pick an author and read my way right through all of his works and then go on to someone else. I also learned to sew, to paint walls and to read blueprints.

We didn't have a car, of course. Even if we had, there would have been the problem of gas rationing coupons. There'd have been only enough for Dad to get to work and back.

There were buses and cabs, however. I used them all the time. I am the only person I know who had a charge account at a taxicab company. This luxury was not your frugal father's usual style. With his work on the night shift, we had few chances at a social life. I think he was afraid if he didn't leave me with a way to get out of the house once in a while, I'd go insane. He was right.

Cookie Time

As I said, not all of baby's first Christmases are memorable. Steve's first Christmas is one I remember, even if he doesn't.

He was born December 18, and this was before hospitals routinely sent new moms and their infants home while the baby was still steaming, so to speak. Then, you stayed in the hospital five to seven days, reading, having both your meals and your child brought to your bed at the proper times – an altogether marvelous vacation for a new mother who seldom took vacations.

This meant bringing him home from the hospital the morning of Christmas Eve. The idea of bringing a new baby into the home on this blessed eve has all sorts of greeting card sentiments attached to it. I planned to do something memorable like putting the babe on a blanket under the lighted tree and calling his two older brothers in to witness our precious gift and building this experience into a Christmas story they would always remember.

I'll always remember the day, even if the three oldest were too young to remember the details and the rest of you weren't born yet.

We arrived home, with the baby, shortly before lunchtime. I was nursing and also suffering from a case of mastitis and feeling awful. But Dad had the night off, so we didn't think we needed extra help and where would we find it on Christmas Eve anyway, with parents and other relatives busy with their own holiday plans.

Sometime during the afternoon a plague swept through the house cutting down everyone in the place except Dad. It could have been food poisoning from the oyster stew I insisted he make, and he didn't eat because he doesn't care for it. Who knows? Anyway, he always said it was HIS most memorable Christmas, making me wonder since then what he thought about some of the others.

Dad spent the rest of Christmas Eve and most of Christmas Day changing bedding, washing clothes, rushing two small boys into the bathroom and locating enough beside buckets for two very sick little boys and nursing mother who suspected she was dying and leaving him to do this for the rest of his life.

He also had to tramp out in the cold searching out bottles and the makings of formula and some medicine for my mastitis. The only thing he didn't have to do was cook Christmas dinner. Nobody was well enough to eat and he didn't have time.

But we were not lonesome. A steady stream of company flowed through the house for two days; friends and relatives who dropped in to see the new baby - friends and relatives who brought cookies.

About every hour on the hour someone would tiptoe in smiling and saying, "I knew you probably didn't have time to bake this year, so I baked for you." And then he, or she or they would add a batch of cookies to the collection in the kitchen.

They stepped around the buckets, ignored the laundry hanging in the kitchen and basement, pretended not to notice everyone in the house was on the critical list and left us with the reassurance that, "If there's anything I can do to help, let me know."

But they left cookies. We needed tender loving care. Dad needed a nap and a meal. I needed someone to feed and bathe the baby. Herb and Ralph needed to be cleaned up. So did the entire house.

But everyone brought cookies and left feeling they had done their Christmas good deed for the year by bringing the couple with the new baby a box of cookies.

The Christmas of the Puppy

First Christmases are not always momentous. Herb's was because it managed to arrive in the middle of a major war and was directly affected by that war. But several of you children have contributed to my list of impressive Christmas memories; however…there was the Christmas of the Puppy.

I don't like dogs. Dad sort of liked them, but he was never a dog nut, thank heaven, and had far too much sense to add puppy confusion to a house with three small boys in it. But that year, someone, who mistakenly thought every boy should have a dog, gave us this untrained little black pup. It was a big hit with everyone – except me, of course.

The puppy wasn't cute or bright or appealing. It had only one function besides eating. You could locate him by following puddles and poopy piles anywhere in the house. Neither Dad nor I had any idea of how to housebreak a dog. Some suggested spanking the puppy with a rolled-up newspaper and putting him outside. This was supposed to give the pup the idea the puddling and pooping are activities to be done outdoors. Nothing was said about how to convince an eight-week old puppy that and icy porch on a sub-zero night is an ideal bathroom.

Anyway this is how it went. The tree was up and decorated – no easy task with three boys ages 2, 4, and 8 getting revved up for Christmas Eve and stocking hangings, not to mention mopping up puddling pooch every 15 minutes. Then Dad decided it was time we undertook the Housebreaking of The Dog. Dad's timing was not good. The dog puddled. Dad whacked it with the newspaper he conveniently prepared for the occasion and rubbed the dog's nose in the puddle, causing Ralph to gag and throw up on the floor. Ralph was a sensitive child and it didn't take much to make him gag.

The puppy was banished to the back porch to yelp and consider his evil ways. Herb decided he had a cruel father and announced he was leaving home, forever. He slammed the front door and ran down the street, minus coat or cap. Ralph, having finished tossing his cookies on the rug, was also upset with his cruel father. The beautiful, gentle boy who rarely got upset about anything had reached his breaking point. To show us how mad he was, HE pushed over the Christmas tree. Steve, age 2, watched his family in big-eyed horror. This was not the "nice hanging up your stockings for Santa Claus" we'd been telling him about for several weeks. He dropped his blankie, took his thumb out of his mouth and began to shriek and sob.

Cruel Father grabbed a sweater and dashed out to find his oldest son – heaven knows why. This left Crazy Mother, who survived the fallen tree, the collective messes made by Ralph and the pup (now barking its heart out on the back porch) and her hysterical youngest son, and began to laugh. She was still laughing, holding her sides, wiping her eyes, rolling around on the couch when Cruel Father stalked in, his oldest son in tow. Oldest son observed that he was cold and tired out and thought he should go to bed. It was a good idea. Ralph, shocked by his terrible deed, and being the smart kid that he was, even at age 4, retreated to his room. Steve wrapped his blankie around his head and went back to sucking his thumb.

You probably want to know how it all ended, but I can't remember, probably because it took me so long to stop laughing. I laughed as we righted the tree, I roared as we cleaned up the messes, I howled as I locked the dumb puppy in the basement for the night. Dad went off to bed, but not before delivering a long monologue about why any man in his right mind would get married and have a family. I assured my oldest son that Santa was going to stop at our house anyway, even if mama was crazy and daddy swore.

Cat vs tree

I love the TV holiday movie "Christmas Story" because it reminds me of when my sons were around the age of the boys in the story, set back in the 1950s. Also reminds my older sons of their childhood. "Just one thing though," I said the other day as we discussed the show. "I really think we were a bit classier than the Parkers. Son gave me a look, a long thoughtful look, possibly thinking of a tactful way to say what was he was thinking.; He sighed, waited another moment, then gently said, "No, mom. We weren't." Which brings me to the story of the Year the Cat killed the Christmas tree. It begins two weeks before Christmas.

In previous years, Dad and the two older boys drove to the corner lot that sold fresh trees each year while I stayed home tending the current toddlers and babies. There was usually one or two — or even three. Together he the boys chose "good tree" and dragged it home. Once inside, the kids and I took our places on couch and chair to watch Dad put up the tree, anchored it with wires to the opposing walls of the bay window in our living, protecting the tree from being toppled by climbing toddlers. By the time we finished Dad's part of the tree ceremony was pretty well finished, and the tree ready to trim a But it was bed time for the children, so that part of the Christmas tradition was reserved for the following night. Then the rest of the continued the tradition, Dad bought and brought home the tree.

It stopped the night Dad came home from work unusually late. He came home, walking into the kitchen with this big sappy grin on his face, I wondered for a moment if he'd stopped at a bar on the way home. Later, kind of wished he had. "Have I got a surprise for you," he told the kids and me. "It's out in the trunk, and I need a little help getting it in the house, it's a pretty big box."

The pretty big box contained the latest thing in artificial trees called an Evergleam tree, a huge Christmas tree-shaped fluff of aluminum branches. No more going down to the corner lot to buy a tree every year. No more stringing unreliable lights, or in fact that was according to the flyer that came with the tree. No more hanging ornaments or vacuuming up pine needles every day.

"So what can do you to it?" the five-year-old whined. "Well, Dad said, "you can look at it. That's all. You don't have to do anything but look.

The tree does it all. "Nice, huh?" So we looked, and listened. What we saw and heard was a revolving tree that turned around and around, as a built-in music box in the base played "Silent Night." For color, two revolving lamps sat on the floor and cast a variety of colors on the branches as the tree turned." Worst of all, it stood in a huge bay window close to the sidewalk so all the neighbors had three different views.

Dad was delighted with his new toy, but he the only one. The children were unhappy over not hanging ornaments or having a green tree that came from the tree lot... Dad was sure they'd come to love it as much as he did. I thought it was the most tasteless gosh-awful item to ever appear in our house. The delight he took in his purchase, and his failure to notice the lack of delighted shrieks, kept me from saying so. I didn't want to hurt his feelings by saying it was the most gosh awful tackiest thing I'd ever seen. Luv, the cat agreed. He didn't care whose feelings he hurt. The tree was hate at first sight. He slunk around the thing, fur inflating him to twice his size, snarling, hissing, growling and jumping at the revolving music box. Finally he appeared to give up. With a baleful "You will pay and pay dearly for his insult," look at Dad, he left the living room for a nap on some kid's bed.

With no lights to string, no ornaments to hang, the rest of us just sat there watching the tree go round and round, at floor lights revolving on the floor turning the tree from red to green and back. It was hypnotic, as was the endless "Silent Night." A different carol once in a while would have been nice. Dad did what he could to generate some enthusiasm without success. It was a long Christmas Eve. I put the kids to bed, got into my jammies and joined Dad still staring at the tree. By even he had run of things to say about the time and work it would save at Christmas, particular for hm. We went to bed.

Next morning was Saturday; Dad got up to restart the tree and the revolving lights. The rest of us awoke slightly altered version of "Silent Night." Some notes were mysteriously missing here and there. A few lower branches of the tree were crooked and showed definite signs of having been attacked. Luv was nowhere to be seen. Only an empty food bowl let us know we even had a cat.

As evening approached, I caught him crouched by the tree, tail flailing, chattering. I yelled "Bad cat. He fled but not before a lightening thrust of a paw swatted the music box, causing further damage. He'd hide at night then come out while we asleep to battle the tree then retired to for the day to nap to somebody's bed — resting up for the nighttime tree battle.

We tried putting him in the basement for the night and learned the true meaning of the word "caterwauling," shrieks and meows from the depths of hell. I let him out so we could get some sleep and he'd disappear to somewhere in our 10-room house. Ever try to find a cat? But each day was the same. Each morning we'd get up to find further evidence of the war the Christmas tree. In one week the revolving music "Silent Night" was reduced to an occasional "plink" and finally stopped revolving altogether as did the aluminum. The two revolving lights were usually toppled and they also had given up. And so had the family.

We still had a week left before Christmas we surrendered, Saturday morning, and time for Dad to say, "You know it's either the tree or Luv, and the kids will hate me forever if we ditch the cat. What do say the boys and I go out and see if we can still find a good green tree? He did and they did.

And we watched while Dad took the aluminum tree and revolving lights out to the garage, and put up the tree. We dragged out the lights and ornaments, lit then sat down to admire the best Christmas ever. Luv came strolling out, inspected the tree, and with a satisfied gurgle a spot on the back of the sofa, behind me. I tipped my head back and whispered in his ear, "Thank you, Luv." He responded with a soft "Meow," "you're welcome.

Family doesn't celebrate holidays, it survives them

Somewhere in the United States at this very moment, perhaps right in our own community is an unknown woman who turns me evergreen with envy. Aside from women with full time housekeepers she is the only person on earth of whom I have ever been jealous. She is the lucky girl for whom Christmas will occur just as predicted in the gospel according to House and Garden.

Her gifts will be wrapped in high style, her halls decked in the latest manner with boughs of holly (sprayed gold, no doubt). Her holiday recipes (all gourmet) will turn out to be delicious, then windows will shine and she will not forget anything.

Christmas morning the family will arise from their beds, then children all in ducky red sleepers with their hair neatly combed, and she in her red velvet gown accompanied by her mate, smartly attired in his imported robe. Downstairs the house is clean and elegant, with no evidence of the Christmas Eve eggnog bash, and a king's ransom in gifts await them. Breakfast and dinner will occur without effort and nobody will seem to sweat the cleanup jobs that follow.

For many reasons Christmas around Old House never seem to come off right. We don't celebrate the holidays, we survive them. There was the Christmas I had an abscessed tooth, and the one when five of the children came down with the measles.

Twice we brought new babies home from the hospital which sounds like a marvelous way to celebrate Christmas, until you stop to consider the bottles, laundry and insanely jealous three year olds. But all was not lost. We were cheered by hordes of visiting in-laws who dropped in to say how sorry they were for us…being in such a mess and all. And by everyone who gave us all their old cookies.

Our Christmas snapshots aren't so good either. There is a tree and the beautiful, photogenic children gathered with their toys, and always this crabby looking woman sitting in their midst. People wonder who she is, why she is in the picture and what ails her. Is she sick? Didn't she get anything for Christmas? Has she ever combed her hair? Why is she wearing that old bathrobe on Christmas morning?

Truth is that mystery woman isn't really crabby. She is in a stupor having gotten only one hour of sleep after spending Christmas Eve doing two weeks work and staying up all night to wrap gifts and trim the tree. Her husband isn't in much better shape, but he's the only one in the family who can operate the camera so nobody every finds this out. But this Christmas is going to be different, and nobody is going to take my picture until I've has at least one cup of coffee.

Chapter 14: Newsworthy

Gay Bob faces bias in doll land

In case you missed the news story last week, Barbie's circle of doll acquaintances may soon be widened to include "Gay Bob," an anatomically correct male doll who comes equipped with his own closet.

With Gay Bob is a booklet explaining to kids why Bob needs a closet and how important it is for his new owner to get him out of it. The manufacturer is certain Gay Bob will catch on in the Midwest as he claims he has in the East.

For what it's worth, and it could be quite a bundle if you spend the money on him, Gay Bob is expected to join G.I. Joe and Ken, if not in the closet, at least under the Christmas tree.

My biggest objection to the whole affair is not so much that someone thought of it. More, it's the waste of money. A cheaper way, less profitable to toy manufacturers and sellers, would be to simply let the news seep out through the 10-and-under set that Ken, or one of his buddies, was not what he said he was all these years and then fix him his own closet.

My other thought is -- why bother at all? Everyone knows mothers buy Barbie dolls for the sole purpose of teaching their daughters that girls are expected to be sexy, beautiful, wear expensive clothes, live in luxury and drive expensive sports cars until they marry and cease to be dolls.

Ken and G.I. Joe dolls are purchased for a variety of reasons. Ken and his friends are needed to escort Barbie and her friends to the disco. G.I. Joe dolls allow boys to act out their most violent male fantasies by letting G.I. Joe and his buddies kill each other.

My daughters owned Ken and G.I. Joe dolls for the sole purpose of keeping their little brother out of their hair when they played with Barbie. They'd send Joe off to "work" or to "war" (where hopefully he'd be killed in action) and this took him out of the game.

Do you know where Gay Bob would fit into this Barbie society? He'd be an outcast. It took all kinds of promoting to get parents to let black dolls into the Barbie set, let alone gays. Bob himself would have a terrible time. Little kids would force him to pass as a heterosexual by putting him in a G.I. Joe suit and sending him out to be killed -- worse, having to date Barbie instead of Ken.

And this is only the beginning. Equality being what it is, soon there'll be a Lesbian Lucy who will need a girlfriend and soon it'll be a status thing to have the only Barbie crowd on the block with its own gay community.

If you're sold on the idea but don't want to spend the money and you've already got a sizeable collection of 11-inch dolls in the toy chest, take heart. All you need to do is start a few nasty rumors and chuck some of them in the closet.

How you do this is your problem. I've already been more helpful than I probably should have been. After all, my kids are past the Barbie stage -- thank heaven.

What would you do if Jesus joined your church?

What would you do if Jesus joined your church? Would His presence at the worship services create any problems for your pastor? Would He influence the sermons? Would He really fit in with the rest of the congregation? He was very poor. What kind of financial contributor would He have made? He was not a doctor or a business man, only a humble worker. Could He be elected to your church committee? And if He was could He possibly understand the complexities of running a church?

Suppose He came to a meeting of a church organization and made His friendship for everyone there apparent, as He would do. Would you introduce Him around and make Him feel welcome? Or might you tend to dismiss him as a pushy newcomer trying to horn in on your special little crowd?

Having Him get up in discussion groups and say things like "Love one another as I have loved you," or "Love your neighbor as yourself," could touch off some sticky problems in some churches. And what if someone were curious enough to ask Him, "Who is my neighbor?" What would you do about His answer?

Someone once said that Jesus was the most attractive person who ever lived. Furthermore He didn't seem to care who He hung around with. Consider for a moment the kind of people who might follow Him into your church…the very poor, the sick and crippled, the distressed…the sinners. Could you make room for them?

Would some of the things He talked about be considered a little "far out" for the rest of the congregation? Would the members regard

Him as a rebel in His thinking, an "ultraliberal" or a voice of hope for those who have none? Would you want Him as a personal friend who would visit you in your home, and you in His? Would you introduce Him to your friends and business associates? Or would you consider Him and oddball, beneath you socially and decide it wouldn't be worth the scorn of the group to risk knowing this "different" man?

Is it possible that He could be absorbed into the church because the ideas He expressed were already in practice?

Would His presence in the congregation be a cause for rejoicing because the Christianity He lived was already there?

Think about it for a while. What would you really do if He joined your church? Do you think He'd fit in?

Chapter 15: Random Thoughts

All about Little Girls

There isn't much difference at first, since they seem to be mostly sleeping and eating. But baby girls tend to be a bit more flower-like and delicate and this gets more noticeable as time passes.

Very tiny girls fall into many categories and are simply crazy about anything which belongs to their mother. They may be Perfume Spillers, Powder Dumpers, Lipstick Smearers or Mascara Scribblers. They are fond of swathing themselves in your fluffy nylon nightgowns and careening down the street in your best shoes. Little girls are also Daddy Flirters, Grandpa Getters and Mama Melters.

When you are feeling ill they will bring you lukewarm coffee in doll cups and peanut butter crackers. Their maternal instincts are powerful and they will mother anything from a wilted tulip to a tired horse. Little girls are marvelous companions. You can find out everything that happens in school which the little boys won't talk about. They love to gossip and their candid observations of their absent playmates will sometimes curl your hair.

Little girls smell like flowers all of the time, even when they are dirty. They do not mind wearing pants and a T-shirt so long as no other little girl in sight is wearing a dress. And they can see no reason why one should not wear white gloves and a bonnet with blue jeans.

They are most helpful when you do not need help and least cooperative when you do need them. It is not necessary to "teach" them to cook and sew and clean house. Just provide them with the materials and the motivation then turn them loose. Stand by with and offer of occasional help. Say things like, "We're having company. Let's make the house look pretty," or "It's Daddy's birthday. We can make him a surprise dinner. You peel the carrots and I'll fix the biscuits."

Get dressed up and go to lunch together. Begin when they are very little to talk with them about many things. Be truthful about what you expect of them.

Teach them to be gentle, brave, honest, loving and humorous, for these are the things they will need to be as women. Then one day they will be grown up, sun crowned and lovely with little girls of their own. And you will find yourself wondering why it took so little time.

Money Can Be Happiness - Especially if you're 4 Years Old

What if you were four years old right now and you have two pennies, and there was a store around the corner? Well there is a grocery store around the corner from our house. And last year they had some purple gumballs for sale, a penny each, and one summer the store sold 8,000 of them. Presumably the purple bubblegum was sold to children within walking distance of the store. Think of it; 8,000 grape-flavored gumballs chomped up and blown into bubbles in just one small sector of our great city.

On the candy counter in this store is a sign, "Don't Just Stand There, Buy Something." But a large share of the penny customers can't read, and all of them are bent upon buying. According to Vicki Gardner, who runs the store, the biggest seller for a penny is bubblegum. Number 2 is a red licorice whip. Close behind are penny suckers and pretzel sticks.

If the first of the big spenders becomes jaded on bubble gum a red licorice, he can try black licorice or chocolate covered caramel rolls for a change. Or he can ruin his teeth on peach-stones at three for a penny or cherry rolls. Or how about a jawbreaker in a choice of four lovely colors? Many of these items were popular when we were children and still sell for a penny. Others have gone up a cent.

One of my old favorites, licorice cigarettes, has become a victim of inflation and gone up to two cents. Another favorite of mine no longer on sale around here was a penny sucker called a BB Bat. It was a taffy-like candy that defied both chewing and sucking and seemed to be shatterproof. I rather imagine it is now used as a bonding material in the building of freeways. Another penny item that enchanted me was a tiny tin pink candy-filled skillet that came with its own wee spoon.

Five-cent candy bars are getting smaller. I'm glad I found this out. For a while I was afraid I was just getting bigger. Plain or with almonds the big sellers are still chocolate bars, and bars with nougat and caramel centers. Mint bars also are popular at the store around the corner. Once, for some reason the youngsters staged a run on cough drops, black and cherry. The store just couldn't keep up with the demand. Suddenly, and just as mysteriously, the cough drop fad passed. One fine day just nobody wanted cough drops.

The corner store does not exist in the suburbs, where running out of cigarettes is a major disaster. But our inner city corner store we regard as a second pantry. It is the first place each child learns to walk unattended when he has a penny. Who says money can't buy happiness?

Madame Butterfly should have lived in '70s

A tear jerker is a tear jerker even after 70 years. That's why I cried my eyes out at the Sunday evening performance of Puccini's grand old weeper set to music, "Madame Butterfly."

It doesn't take much to make me cry. Butterfly was much -- too much, in fact, for one who sheds tears at strangers' funerals, parades, graduations and all of the sad parts in "The Walton's."

But even as I wept over the way that jerk of a navy lieutenant made all of those promises to Butterfly and then left her to support their child, little things began to surface in my mind.

Butterfly was faithful, never dreaming she was only a one-night stand in the affections of Pinkerton. Her suicide was a real four-Kleenex jonnie. But, I fantasized, I'll bet the real drama came afterward when he and his other wife (the one he married after he returned to the United States) got together to talk things over.

That steamship trip home with the child of Pinkerton's other wife must have been a hairy one. Of course, when you saw the snow job he did on Butterfly in the first act, it wasn't hard to suppose he'd flim-flam Kate too.

It's also not hard to understand why the opera was not performed much during World War II. After all, when the bad guy, the heel, the trifler of with the affections of innocent womanhood is an American Navy officer, it gets sticky when the innocent woman being trifled with is "the enemy." I thought about that too, when all about me were concentrating on the music.

The plot of Madame Butterfly is downhill all the way from the moment at the end of the first act when Pinkerton tells his bride that he's moving out in the morning, to the death scene at the end. It's a three-hour trip from depression to suicide -- literally. So don't see it if you want to be cheered up.

Another thought which sprang to mind between my sobs was this: Madame Butterfly wouldn't have been so badly used had she lived in the 1970s. Women, even Japanese women, are a lot more savvy than they were in Nagasaki, Japan back in 1900 when Pinkerton came sailing (steaming, I guess is the correct word) into the harbor all dressed up in his white uniform.

Now she'd insist on a marriage contract, an allotment as a serviceman's wife and his insurance benefits. Trifling today is big business, particular if one happens to be the "triflelee."

A modern scenario might have Butterfly marrying the prince, who, it turns out, is president of the Yakzuki camera and computer company. Pinkerton would return with his second wife and Butterfly would have him thrown in jail for non-payment of child support, bigamy and breach of contract.

Kate Pinkerton, on learning her husband had skipped out on his first wife without bothering with a divorce, would go first to a marriage counselor and then to an attorney.

"Pink, old boy," she'd say, (when Pink got out of jail, which might take a while) "you blew it -- you really blew it. When Butterfly's lawyers get through with you, mine will be waiting outside the door."

With which, she'd fly back to the United States, buy a ticket to a singles' cruise with Pinkerton's credit cards and live happily ever after.

The liberation of women may not have done much for operas in which heroines died lingeringly and loudly from lack of love. The thought of what it might have done for Poor Butterfly did a lot for me as I wiped the tears from my eyes at the end of act three.

Hansen Children

Herbert James Hansen 1941

Ralph Wayne Hansen 1945

Stephen Andrew Hansen 1947

John Christopher Hansen 1950

Edward James Hansen 1952-2009

Patricia Ann (Jaime) Hansen 1954

Barbara Sue (Schultz) Hansen
1957-2000

Holly Beth (Tiret) Hansen 1959

Joseph Gerard Hansen 1961

Closing thoughts

Discouraged? Take Time to Look Back August

Never look back, say some wise men. I don't always agree. Sometimes I look back, not on my failures, though I have many of these, but in sheer wonder at my successes. It's like climbing to the top of a hill on a dark night and seeing the lights on the road you traveled sparkling behind you.

How far I have come, even during some of those times when I used to think I was standing still and all the wonderful things of life were rushing by me.

If you are a mother, look back for a while. Maybe the needlepoint you love to do or the sewing you do so well lies tucked in back of the closet because right now you are busy with babies all day and fatigued from getting up too many nights with new infants.

Look back. Look at the needlepoint or the beautiful things you made before and know that the time to create is both behind and ahead and this is just another of those times in your life when it takes all you've got just to row the boat, let alone ponder the beautiful sea around you.

This may sound like a far out allegory, but young mothers who are cleaning up after toddlers all day will not think so.

If nothing else, look back on the miracle of survival; from embryonic nothingness to being able to walk to a window and look up at the sky. In spite of everything which may have happened that didn't, there is a wonder about having come from then to now.

Sometimes people who are very old look back and see the difficult, often meaningless hard work that kept them and their families alive. But along the way were golden loaves of bread in the kitchen, cellars of canned goods like jewels in the darkness. There were times when the crops were good, when work was good.

And there were the children born strong and perfect in spite of a thousand and one biological reasons why they should not have been born at all.

Sometimes what we are doing seems meaningless and endless and often forever. I remember when my typewriter gather dust under my bed while I nursed babies and washed diapers and tried to keep the house clean.

Then I would read the things I had written before and knew that I would do this again. Meantime I had another important job to do, and gave it all I had. I'm glad I did now that I can see my children grown up to be what I had hoped they would be.

And this is why I often look back. I always wished for a clear road and a level one. I never got it. But when I look back I realize it didn't matter.

Betty in her happy place – her office